Transforming
AMERICA
from the Inside Out

Transforming AMERICA
from the Inside Out

Kay Coles James
with David Kuo

ZondervanPublishingHouse
Grand Rapids, Michigan

A Division of HarperCollinsPublishers

Transforming America
Copyright 1995 © by Kay Coles James

Requests for information should be addressed to:
  Zondervan Publishing House
  Grand Rapids, Michigan 49530

Library of Congress Cataloging-in-Publication Data:

James, Kay Coles.
    Transforming America : from the inside out / Kay Coles James :
with David Kuo.
        p. cm.
ISBN 0-310-48440-5
        1. United States—Religion—1960- 2. Religion and politics—United
States. 3. Conservatism—Religious aspects—Christianity.   4. Religious
fundamentalism—United States. 5. Afro-Americans—Religion. I. Kuo,
David. II. Title.
BR526.J36 1994
269'.0973—dc20   94-24974
                                                                        CIP

Edited by Lyn Cryderman and Mary McCormick

Printed in the United States of America

95 96 97 98 99 00 / ❖ DC / 10 9 8 7 6 5 4 3 2 1

This edition is printed on acid-free paper and meets the American National
Standards Institute Z39.48 standard.

Contents

Introduction 7

Part 1

1. The Election 17
2. "Cultural AIDS" 31
3. Yes, We Can! 41
4. Individuals 49
5. Families 55
6. The Community 65
7. Churches 73
8. Education 83

Part 2

9. Abortion 99
10. Homosexuality in America 111
11. Racism 123
12. Poverty 139
13. Time Is Not a Measure of Success 151
    Epilogue 161

Introduction

[I]f you preach the gospel in all aspects with the exception of the issues which deal specifically with your time, you are not preaching the gospel at all.

—MARTIN LUTHER

Recently, an old African proverb has been making the rounds: "It takes a village to raise a child." Its message seems clear: We are all in this together. One can just imagine all of the different segments of society gathering round the innocent babe, protecting it, teaching it, loving it. And as the child grows, the "village" grows with it. The "village" is there to guide the child on life's path. The "village" is there for the child should the child fall. The village is where the children will eventually marry and have children of their own, completing a cycle of harmony and knowledge.

It seems that the more our families fail, the more violence grows, the more our schools forget, the more this old proverb is repeated. Conference after conference, talk after talk, and book after book have discussed the importance of the village in raising children. It is really quite simple, we are told, if only we would cede parental control to the village, all would be well. Children would no longer grow up insecure or worried; they would be well-adjusted, well-developed, and full of healthy self-esteem. What a wonderful world it would be. . . .

But the village cannot raise a child. Children don't belong

to the community. Children belong to the parents who tuck them in at night, wipe away their tears, feed them their meals, and answer their questions. If the past thirty years have taught us anything, it is that stable, intact, two-parent families are the foundation of a healthy village.

But a healthy village requires more. For it is in the village that the child will live, play, learn, and grow. The village is the theater where much of the child's life will be played out. It is the village that can ultimately complement or undermine the lessons and values of home. Consider:

What would happen to the village if churches taught that truth does not exist? That God is really just the creation of a species of animals desperate to justify their own existence? That *what* you believe does not have to impact *how* you behave? My guess would be that that church would have very little relevance to the lives of the citizenry—that people would go elsewhere to find meaning.

What would happen to the village if we came to believe that the type of family that raises a child just is not very important? My guess is that we would gradually see the diminishment of the two-parent family, as well as a rapid rise in the number of births out of wedlock, abortions, and abused and abandoned children.

What would happen if our public schools started teaching that children should be judged not by what they learn in reading, writing, and arithmetic but by how they get along with the other little children and how well they display the attitudes and behaviors that the schools decide are important? My guess is that our children would grow up preoccupied about their self-esteem but ultimately being frustrated because they could not do basic math or read above a sixth-grade level.

What would happen, in our village, if the most important

institution of society, the one everyone depends on, were the government? My guess is that government would grow and grow and grow. The government center would dominate the center of our villages, taking over more and more aspects of people's lives—perhaps even telling them which doctors they can see and what kind of treatment they may have.

What would happen if all of these things occurred at the same time? My belief is that today in America, we are seeing the answer to that question played out in front of our eyes. We are seeing the diminishment of our corporate ability to fight off societal infections such as violence, hopelessness, hatred, promiscuity, and despair. There has been much talk about the "Culture Wars." According to many, we have *all* been called to action—one camp against another—a fight for God and country!

I believe their diagnosis is incorrect. We are not currently in a cultural war. Instead, we are *a* culture, one comprised of many different segments, *a* culture that is very sick, *a* culture that is very near death. The source of our illness is not a war but a disease. It is called *Cultural AIDS*.

Just as the HIV virus attacks those parts of the human body that defend it against disease, so, too, has this cultural virus attacked what de Tocqueville called the "values-generating" or values-defending institutions of society—the vital components of the village. Systematically, steadily, we have seen the most important institutions of society weakened. Churches, schools, colleges, universities, businesses, communities, families, and individuals are all less alive in 1995 than they were ten, fifteen, thirty years ago. While, for all the obvious reasons, we certainly do not want to go back thirty years, we do want to keep those things that were good, honest, virtuous, and sustaining. Those things that should remain the same yesterday, today, and tomorrow. Those things that give us hope and meaning. Like the "opportunistic infections" that infect the human body, the village is being savaged by infections that numb the senses—murders, rapes, thefts, cheating, lying, rampant promiscuity, and moral relativism.

For those who doubt, watch just one segment of CNN Headline News. Flip through just one issue of *Time* or *Newsweek*. Page through just one edition of your morning newspaper. Listen to the morning news on your radio when you drive to work or clean the house. And if you want to see what is to come, listen to some of the songs on the radio. Watch some of the movies in the multiplex. I guarantee that what you will see, hear, and read will frighten you. And well it should.

To those who say that the solutions to our problems lie somewhere in the political arena, somewhere in the economic arena, somewhere in just educating people, somewhere in the crime bill, somewhere in health-care reform, or somewhere in public policy—I say that the reality could not be more different or more difficult!

The solutions are not political. Politics is but a subset of the culture and will only affect certain areas. It will not fundamentally change this country, or bring it back to where it needs to be. I wish it could.

Just as the HIV researchers of today are seeking ways to build up the T-cells that prevent infectious diseases from attacking the body, so, too, we must seek to rebuild *our* immune system—the village. That means some pretty tough things for all of us. It means that we must be people of virtue. It means that we need to restore the family, the churches, the schools, the businesses, and the community. The bottom line is this: We need to get up out of our easy chairs—to love and discipline our children, be involved in our schools, be faithful to the call of God in our lives, be ethical in our businesses, and be involved in our communities. Unfortunately for us, doing these things is *the only way* we can reclaim our culture and rebuild our corporate village and therefore our country . . . from the inside out.

When I was growing up, there used to be a sense of community in which neighbor looked out for neighbor—where people cared for each other. There was a time in my community when, if I did something wrong, my next-door neighbor would discipline me, and then when Mom got home, she would "talk" to me as well. That community was part of our immune system.

Another part of our immune system was that Grandma used to take us to church every Sunday morning, where we would go to Sunday school *and* listen to the sermon. There we would learn the difference between right and wrong. That church was a part of our immune system.

Dr. Tony Evans is a very large, very imposing, and very godly minister from Dallas, Texas. In June 1944, when addressing the Southern Baptist Pastors' Conference in Orlando, he summed up our cultural state and our cultural solutions in a way I am not likely to forget. He said,

> If you are a messed-up individual, contributing to a messed-up family, causing a messed-up church, resulting in a messed-up neighborhood, leading to a messed-up city and your city is in a state, then you gonna have a messed-up state. If you are a messed-up individual, contributing to a messed-up family, resulting a messed-up church, causing a messed-up neighborhood, leading to a messed-up city, resulting in a messed-up state, and your state is in a country, then you gonna have a messed-up country. If you are a messed-up individual, resulting in a messed-up family, leading to a messed-up church, resulting in a messed-up neighborhood, causing a messed-up city, contributing to a messed-up state, in a messed-up country, and your country is in the world,

then you gonna have a messed-up world. So if you want a better world made up of better countries, and composed of better states, inhabited by better cities, led by better neighborhoods, illuminated by better churches, composed of better families, we better create a better generation of young people through our churches.

When you look back at the major cultural shifts in our history and the social reform in our country, most times they were started by one person, or one small group of people. It does not take that many people.

The effort needed to rebuild the village is not one for the weak or the timid. We are engaged in a life-or-death situation that will require people who can go down to the water and not take their eyes off the battle. *With Gideon, it only took three hundred.*

If ever we feel lonely, deserted, and afraid, that's okay. There are no promises that the struggle will be easy or painless; in fact, it is probable that it will be none of the above. I was once reminded when I was considering a rather demanding job opportunity that God's perfect will for my life is not necessarily a comfort zone!

The prophet Nehemiah reminds us to start with individuals and to start with families. I am convinced that if I saved every at-risk youth in America and lost one of my own, I would have failed in God's primary mission for my life. The kind of individual who is going to be required to engage in this battle is the kind who understands right from wrong, truth from lies, and the nobility of a life of courage, valor, honesty, and integrity.

The government has not yet invented a program, a piece of legislation, or a department that can give hope to a disconnected urban youth, that can help a husband love his wife, that can teach a child honesty and integrity, or that can bring youth face-to-face with the person of Christ. That is because such a program does not exist. The only place where such a program can happen is in our homes, and in our schools, and in our churches. That is what this book is about.

Part 1

Chapter One

The Election

The letterhead on the stationery said, "Executive Office of the President," somehow implying that we were located in the White House—at the heart of all that was happening. The reality could not have been more different. I stood at the window in the "drug czar's" office, located above a McDonald's, two blocks from 1600 Pennsylvania Avenue, and wondered what was happening there. How perfectly the situation reflected the *myth* of "inside the beltway" life—the myth that those working in or even near marble buildings in the nation's capital know everything that happens before anyone else.

As Associate Director of the White House Office of National Drug Control Policy, I was deeply involved in developing and articulating drug policy. On November 4, 1992, however, I had other things on my mind. It was election day, and I wondered what the *White House* knew. I wondered whether President Bush, down in Houston, knew the results of the day. I wondered whether the expensive exit polling that gave the campaign early and accurate indications of the voting trends had already concluded the day's results. Had a message already been delivered to the president? Had Jim Baker approached him and said, "Mr. President, I'm sorry, but we're not going to be able to pull this one off"? If so, when had it come? Had it been late morning, after lunch, dinnertime? How had he taken the news?

Those were the thoughts racing through my mind as I stared out the window of my office. My executive assistant came in and said that a reporter was on the line and wanted to know my plans for the evening. He was doing a story about people involved in the campaign and their election-night activities. Mine would prove too boring. All I wanted to do was go home with Charles, round up the children, go out to dinner, return home, and go to bed.

It had been a long campaign and I was tired. As an individual and as a family, I knew that we had done everything we could to win this battle, but I was also frustrated. The days and weeks leading up to the election had been difficult. My confirmation had been held up for months by certain Democratic members of the Senate Judiciary Committee because they wanted me to promise not to campaign for President Bush. Nevertheless, I managed to be involved in a number of projects. Besides my speech at the Republican National Convention in Houston, I was involved in a salute to the president for his black appointees. More than two thousand African-American people paid $250 a piece to honor the man who had appointed more African-Americans to positions of power than any other president in history. Amidst the full-gospel choir and jazz quartet, I saw the full-Washington press corps. Not one story appeared in the national media the following day, however. Throughout the campaign I ran into the "media juggernaut"—the absolute unwillingness of most of those in the media to give President Bush credit for anything. They were, it seemed, determined to bolster all of his negative stereotypes. Unfortunately, the media juggernaut was not the only obstacle the president faced in his attempt to be reelected.

Those surrounding the president knew the pro-family issue was important but did not know how to frame the issue, did not know how to get the message across, and did not want to allow into their inner circle those who did. The result was the "family values debacle." Many political pundits and many members of the Bush-Quayle '92 team have said that family values lost the election for President Bush. That is revisionist history. All of the polling coming out of Houston showed a measurable bump from the convention that had brought the president within four to eight points of Governor Clinton. The problem with the "values debate" was that those on the "inside" appeared to view it as merely another political tool or lever to be used, not a principle on which to take a stand. The result was a caricature of what the pro-family agenda was about. Although my husband, Charles, and I had headed up the pro-family coalition, we, and others such as Gary Bauer and William Bennett, could only do so much. We had traveled all over the nation, we had done the phone banks, we had done the mailings, and we had done the public-service announcements. We even had a last-minute pro-family video—highlighting the gains for families and children under the Bush administration and promising more of the same in the future—sent to twenty-five thousand pastors. It landed on most of their doorsteps two days after the election, which says something about why we lost.

Looking around the office, I saw all sorts of attitudes and emotions on display, especially among the political appointees. On the one hand, there was Pat Casal, the eternal optimist. All day long she refused to give up. "We're going to pull this thing off," she would say. "We're going to make it happen." On the other hand, there was the group who had given up long ago.

They had started working on résumés, renewing private-sector contacts months ago. For them, the election would only serve to confirm their own long-held conclusions. My own attitude was somewhat pious. I had adopted an "I'm trusting God, and this is all up to Him, anyway" approach. I knew that we had worked our hearts out and that the rest was up to Him.

Regardless of the outcome of the election, I sensed that it would be an evening of great emotion for the James family. This was, after all, the first presidential ballot cast by our oldest child, Chuck, and it was eighteen-year-old Elizabeth's first experience in being involved in a national campaign, not just learning about one in a classroom. As was our custom, Charles, who worked around the corner from me, met me in the lobby of my building. Because of our proximity, we commuted together almost every day. I cherished these times with him. We had more quality time together as a couple than most families ever do because we were trapped together in a slow-moving vehicle for a couple of hours each day. Charles and I would occasionally wonder whether this "quality" time was all that it was cracked up to be, but the time still afforded us the opportunity to resolve problems and issues that faced us both individually and as a couple. That day, traffic was unusually heavy, and our conversation was unusually quiet as we both reflected on the changes that were almost certainly headed our way, both as a family and as citizens of the country. We stopped by our house, picked up the children, and headed out for some "comfort food," something everyone needed that night.

Charles and I tried to prepare the children for what was coming. We explained to them both the political and the spiritual realities. "Politics is fun, and it matters, but it also has its highs and its lows," we said, "and this will probably be one of the lows." More important, we tried to relay to them God's sovereignty. "God is not only in control of our personal lives, He is also in control of the affairs of nations."

We arrived home at about 8:30 and promptly turned on the TV. Returns were just starting to trickle in. Kentucky was the first state to report. Deep down I held out hope that all of the polls had been wrong, that once people got into the voting booths, they would pull the lever for President Bush. But reality was sorely different. One state after another came in against the president, and it soon became clear that there was no hope for victory that evening. We were all remarkably peaceful as we turned in to bed and went to sleep.

The next day dawned with the media's announcing a "new age" and a "mandate for change." Our commute that morning was as quiet as the drive home the night before. With piety still intact, I prepared myself for an office full of rather downtrodden people. I took seriously my role as a leader and prepared for the motivational speech I would give my staff at lunch. Several weeks before the election I had made arrangements, win or lose, to take out to lunch all of the political appointees in my office the day after the election.

Our glum group of twenty arrived at my favorite Chinese restaurant shortly after noon. The group was quiet as we started to eat, and I decided to launch into my speech right away. I told them that first and foremost they should feel proud and that they should remember their accomplishments. I also encouraged them not to be discouraged by the unemployment lines that lay ahead for many of them. They were talented, and I told them that. I then turned to the impending transition that lay ahead of us. I began to prepare them for the massive job of sorting and filing documents, preparing briefing memos and strategy memos—the work of peaceful transition that makes democracy so much more preferable for deposed administrations than a coup.

When halfway through my speech a jubilant group of Democrats entered the restaurant, I cut my remarks short, and the meal continued in relative silence as the reality of our loss began to set in. At that moment, my own optimism, my own piety, suddenly began to slip. In its place was a creeping anger and bitterness—it was no longer easy to be pious .

I began repeating my motivational speech to myself and found that I was no more cheered than any of the other recipients. As the day progressed, my anger and bitterness only increased. The focus of my anger shifted throughout the day—first God, then the Republican National Committee, the campaign, and the country . . . all of the meetings, speeches, late nights, travel, prayer, testimony, and op-eds. . . .

The struggle was rooted in, among other things, the knowledge that the gains in which I had been involved at the drug policy office, at the Department of Health and Human Services, and before that at National Right to Life, would be slowly but surely lost. I had been in Washington nearly twelve years, fighting to make sure that that wall of separation stayed between abortion and family planning—fighting to make sure that at the National Institute of Health and other federal medical facilities all over the country were not performing research and experiments on fetal tissue—fighting to make sure there were people with a high regard for the Constitution sitting on the bench at the Supreme Court and at lower-level courts all across the country. And, of course, there were the issues about which I cared but in which I had not been personally involved— national security, the economy, education . . . and all the work yet undone on issues like health care, welfare reform, and others. Had I realized then what the President-elect would do in some of his first official acts—repeal many pro-life policies by Executive Order and nearly abolish the drug policy office—I would have been even more distraught.

The days and weeks that followed the election went by agonizingly slowly. They were depressing and demoralizing days—days when great fears were realized and great hopes were dashed. They were days of imminent good-byes and not-so-imminent new jobs. They were days in which we all second-guessed ourselves, wondering what we could have done better and how that might have changed things. They were days when the recognition finally set in that this country had completely rejected the goals we were striving for—had rejected the values that I held dear. In effect, they said to us, "You are outta here. Get your stuff and leave." That did not feel good.

At the same time that I was dealing with this, I was dealing with something else that was very, very, very important. There was a young woman ... She and I had become close as a result of our church association. My daughter baby-sat her children. We talked regularly. We had dinner together. We laughed and cried together. She was one of the most remarkable women I had ever known. This woman, no matter where she lived, had an impact on her community. It was really interesting to meet Mindy's friends because these friends seemed always to understand God better, to grow in their relationships, to be involved in their communities—all from having known her.

It was very difficult to deal with the loss of an election. It was even more difficult to deal with the impending loss of a dear friend. Mindy White was in the final stages of breast cancer. Somehow it just did not seem right—a mom with four little children, ages three, six, nine, and eleven.

I had spent many hours talking with reporters, women's groups, and others about the prevention and early detection of a disease that has ravaged so many American women. Now, suddenly, it was no longer a public-affairs program, it was my friend. This was a lesson that I think all policy makers should be forced to study.

I spent many evenings and nights by her bed, talking to her, comforting her, and being comforted by her. She was a woman who reminded me of why I cared for this country and its future. She was a wife and a mother who loved her kids and family enough to be politically involved. She was one of the millions of unsung heroines across the country who wrote the letters to Congress, who called the Senate, who cared enough about her country to invest her time and her energy.

She was also a woman with many questions, facing death. Death has a remarkable way of cutting to what really matters. Mindy and I talked about salvation, about facing our Lord before the judgment seat, about our lives, and about our families. We spent hours speculating about heaven and what a great joy it would be coming into the presence of our Lord.

It was a time of remarkable contrasts for me. The work of the transition continued. During the day I put together briefing books that explained our policies. At night I talked about what was lasting, eternal, and valid. I searched in vain for the relevance of the former and for the wisdom of the latter. I was struggling with the loss of an election during the day and with the loss of a friend in the evening.

All around me there were people who were trying to figure out where they would live after the Inauguration. Would they have to sell their homes? Would they have to move to another part of the country? And there was Mindy struggling with the fact that her life was ending.

During the day, we dealt with children who would be disrupted because they were being taken out of school in the middle of the year. At night I dealt with the grief of a mother who would not see her children grow up.

Every day I would leave the office at about 2:00 P.M. and go out to her house. I would arrive to find this extraordinary woman home-schooling her kids from her bed. I would spend the rest of the day and most of the weekend at her home. On a couple of occasions she looked at me with concern and said, "Kay, how can you leave work every day and do this? Shouldn't you be at work? What's happening? Who's running the country?" I used to look back at her and laugh, saying, "Sweety, this is the period know as the 'transition.' *Nothing* is happening right now. Mindy, there are those who think this is the best government you are ever gonna get. There are scads of people who complain that transitions are too long. I think that maybe they should make them two years." We both laughed a lot to contend with our grief.

As the days dwindled down to the Inauguration, I concluded that there were other places to be than Washington for the beginning of the new Administration. To the rest of the world I could put on my "I'm fine, and isn't democracy great?" face; inside, the thought of being in Washington for the Inauguration was more than I could bear. So days before the Inauguration, we headed for a ski resort just outside Charlottesville, Virginia.

I was looking forward to a few days of sleep, books, snowball fights, and maybe even some sledding. At the time, I forgot that God has a thing for mountains and deserts. It seems that they make perfect places for Him to work with us. So it was for me in the mountains of Virginia. Although we made a pact that we would not watch any of the inaugural activities, we frequently caught each other sneaking a peek at the television. It was nice to be away from the constant din of noise that is a part of life in

Washington or any big city. The fresh air, the rest, the time with family were all medicine for the soul.

Late Sunday night, long after we had all gone to bed, the phone rang. Groggily, I picked it up and mumbled, "Hello?" All I remember hearing is the voice on the other end of the phone, saying, "Mindy went home to be with the Lord." Though long expected, her death was still extraordinarily painful. Her friendship had both encouraged and challenged me, and in her death she managed to confront me again with some painful truths.

It occurred to me that while I was struggling with what was happening on a national level during the day and struggling with what was happening on a personal level with my friend in the evening, somehow what I was seeking from God was right there before me all along.

Those of us who are involved in state or national policy and politics, to use a football analogy, are on defense. We just cover and tackle. They throw the ball up; we swat it down. But you cannot win a game on defense. To win, we need an offensive strategy. Someone must be advancing the ball. That means being engaged, as Mindy was.

As I reflected on Mindy's death and all of its implications, the months of struggling with myself, with the problems of the country, with the new administration, with anger and with bitterness, were finally beginning to make sense. I finally began to get it right. Politics was not the cause of our problems, nor was it the solution—*we* were. I turned to my sleeping husband, elbowed him a couple of times, and said, in a not-too-quiet voice, "Charles, honey, are you awake?" For the next several hours, I struggled mightily with the weight on my heart as my wonderful husband struggled to stay conscious, listening, and supporting.

I grappled again with questions of priorities ... values ...

faith. I finally needed to look at the eternal. What the weeks and months of struggling taught me was that the problems that we face, both as individuals and as a nation, are not primarily political ones; they are spiritual and social as well.

It does not matter how many awful pieces of legislation we block or how many great pieces of legislation we implement. We can have the best justices on the Supreme Court and the best legislators in Congress, but if we as a people are not able to live lives faithful to our Creator, devoted to our families, earnest in our work, and cheerful in our demeanor, all of those political changes will have been for nothing, because we, the people, will have failed.

I really believed, coming into government, that I was going to be a part of helping to shape the course of a nation—that I would be helping take this nation into the next century. I was awed by the responsibility. Someone once said to me, "If you don't get cold chills when you pass the monuments in the morning, if you don't get excited every time you walk into the Oval Office, if you don't realize the awesome responsibility you have when you go up to testify before Senate committees, then Kay, you do not deserve that job." I have to tell you that I arrived in Washington, thinking, *What a responsibility*. I came with high hopes and high expectations. Suddenly, I had a slightly different perspective.

I was coming to realize that the first role of a Christian in government is to ensure that one does no harm. I realized that if we want to make an impact on the culture and shape the course of a nation, the best chance of doing that is individual by individual, family by family, church by church, and community by community, and not necessarily election by election.

While I was very disappointed about what was happening on a national level, God finally showed me through Mindy and through her death that in her very short life she did more to shape the culture, to make an impact on people's lives, and to forge the course of a nation than I had done by being involved in national or state politics.

Shortly before his death, Lee Atwater, the brilliant political strategist, wrote in *Life* magazine about his own struggle with cancer. He wrote that he had finally realized what was temporal and what was eternal, and that only the latter mattered. He wrote,

> I acquired more wealth, power, and prestige than most. But you can acquire all you want and still feel empty. What power wouldn't I trade for a little more time with my family? What price wouldn't I pay for an evening with friends? It took a deadly illness to put me eye to eye with that truth, but it is a truth that the country, caught up in its ruthless ambitions and moral decay, can learn on my time. I don't know who will lead us through the '90s, but they must be made to speak to this spiritual vacuum at the heart of American society, this tumor of the soul.

Lee's analogy was a proper one. He identified the fact that we are struggling with a disease. Unfortunately, our disease is not cancer—it is cultural AIDS. Today, we are a society suffering from a gradual breakdown of our cultural immune system. What threatens us is not a deadly virus but the opportunistic infections that have taken over our weakened cultural immune system. Broken families, uneducated children, moral relativism, these things will not kill us, but they invite the things that will: crime, hopelessness, promiscuity, deceit, and darkness.

I had the privilege of speaking at Mindy's memorial service. I walked to the front of the church, put my hands on the pulpit, and lifted my head. Before me was a sea of people who had been touched by her life. It was amazing to recognize that there was never a neighborhood that she had lived in that someone had not been deeply touched by her. There was never a community in which she was not involved. There was never time for the mush of the afternoon talk shows or soap operas. To Mindy, life was too precious to waste a single moment.

It is Mindy's lesson to me that was the inspiration for this book. From her we can learn much. First, however, we must have the courage to look our country square in the face and see what is going on in our lives, our homes, our churches, and our communities.

We must have the courage to acknowledge that while political change is important, cultural change is essential! It is not either/or, it is both/and. The strategies and skills that many of us know so well in political battles are useless in healing our sick and dying culture. We must transform America from the inside out, starting with you and me.

Chapter Two

"Cultural AIDS"

The safest road to Hell is the gradual one—the gentle slope, soft underfoot, without sudden turnings, without milestones, without signposts.

—C. S. LEWIS

Ladeeta Gaynell Smith's story shows how much darker childhood can be in an age of AIDS, crack, violence, and rampant promiscuity. It was 1984, and in the Cypress Hills housing project there was a relatively new drug called crack. *Ladeeta, who was nine, did not quite understand what was happening in her East New York City neighborhood. The boys who used to be her friends now stood somberly on street corners crowded with people looking to get high. They would warn her if they expected trouble and shoo her into the apartment. The older boys had new jobs for which they carried guns about the vacant lots and abandoned buildings and shot at boys from other projects. Then came the violence. The first ones to die were the boys, her friends like Butch and Pig. But then the violence spread, and she learned to duck for cover when the shoot-outs began. Other friends did not. One girlfriend was shot in the arm. Another died from a gunshot wound to the back.*

In late 1986, her father died—overdose of pills and alcohol. Shortly thereafter, her mother fell to crack. Ladeeta would see her occasionally, dancing and whooping it up in a drug-induced stupor. Ladeeta started running with a gang of girls who beat and robbed other girls for their jewelry and cash. She struggled alone to take care of her two younger sisters. More often than not, she was absent from school. Her first job was holding drugs and cash for a major neighborhood crack dealer.

By 1992, her mother's HIV had become AIDS, and Ladeeta watched helplessly as she deteriorated. Visiting her in a Bronx nursing home, she was haunted by the image of her mother's emaciated body covered with sores. At forty-one, Patricia Smith could no longer recognize her own daughter. In early 1993, her mother died, and Ladeeta was an orphan.

I f we are touched by the pain in our country; if we want to have an impact on our culture; if we truly care, there are certain, defined, things that we must pursue. The first of them is the courage to confront our realities. We must look at our corporate problems objectively, without fear but with resolve. The depth of our problems is astounding, but knowing the enemy is the most important part of defeating it. In this case, the enemy is not a person or a group of people.

Ladeeta's story was but one of ten that ran in a series entitled "Children of the Shadows" in the spring of 1993 in the *New York Times*. Each part of the series focused on one child growing up in an American city. Many of the stories are horrific in the details they present: eleven- and twelve-year-old girls with multiple sexual partners, eleven- and twelve-year-old boys worrying about their own deaths, eleven- and twelve-year-olds who had never known a mother's hug or a father's care. Ladeeta's story is not unusual—neither is it complete. Ladeeta has not ended up as another statistic. In fact, at the writing of the series, she was an eighteen-year-old senior at Boys & Girls High School in Brooklyn, preparing her college applications.

The change in her life, however, was not just the result of an influx of government services or programs. What most changed her life was the love of one woman and one special school. Not all are as blessed:

- On a sticky New York City evening in Crown Heights, a station wagon driven by a Hasidic Jew ran a red light, collided with another car, then jumped the curb and struck two black children, killing one and seriously injuring another. Racial tension was high. Rumors were spread, allegations made, and some blacks said it was racial. Three hours later a group of marauding black youths intent on avenging the deaths stabbed to death Yankel Rosenbaum, a twenty-nine-year-old visiting Hasidic scholar from Australia. Four nights of rioting began and before "calm" was restored 163 people were arrested, 239 people were injured, and 28 police cars were damaged.

- October 1, 1993 was a starlit night in the northern California town of Petaluma. Earlier in the day, twelve-year-old Polly Klaas had finished cleaning her room so her mother would let her invite two girlfriends to sleep over. Following a night of pizza and popsicles in her house on a tree-lined street of a safe middle-class neighborhood, the three girls played a board game and settled down to go to bed. Suddenly, a large bearded man appeared in her doorway, put pillowcases over the heads of the young girls, and took Polly away, never again to be seen alive. That young girl, quietly playing in her own locked house, with her mother asleep in the next room, was abducted and then killed hours later.

- In February 1993, somewhere in the United States, the thirty millionth unborn child was torn from her mother's womb and tossed into the trash. *Thirty million*—a total nearly equivalent to the population of the entire state of California. Thirty million children who will never live and walk and love among us, because someone's "right to choose" was preeminent over another's "right to life."

- *People* magazine hailed it as one of the best shows on TV in 1993. *Time* said it was one of the best new dramatic shows to debut in years. *Fortune* had it on its "hot" list. It won a record number of Emmy Awards. What is "it"? It is *NYPD Blue.* It began its run on September 21, 1993. It has crossed new frontiers of nudity and vulgar language on prime-time television. It was also the hottest show of 1994.

- In December 1993, *60 Minutes* ran an exposé on a homeless shelter in Washington, D.C., whose employees were extorting homeless men and women out of food, clothes, and money. The most disconnected among us, further victims.

- Five-year-old Ray had been coming to school, hungry and cold. It was January 1994, and his teacher wanted to know what was going on. She drove down the street looking for his house—1101, 1103, 1105, a burned-out building, 1109 . . . where was 1107? She got out of the car and walked up and down the street looking for 1107. Suddenly, she saw Ray in the burned-out building that was his home. His mother and father were drug addicts who took what little money they had and spent it on their habits—not on Ray's needs.

The anecdotes are superficial. The realities are even more

frightening. In March 1993 and again in February 1994, William Bennett, the former "drug czar" and Secretary of Education, published the *Index of Leading Cultural Indicators,* "the most comprehensive statistical portrait available on behavioral trends over the last thirty years." His findings:

- a five hundred percent increase in violent crime
- a more than four hundred percent increase in illegitimate births
- a tripling of the percentage of children living in single-parent homes
- a tripling in the teenage suicide rate
- a doubling in the divorce rate
- a drop of almost seventy-five points in SAT scores.

Not too long ago, his findings would have been greeted with smirks and sneers. He would have been accused of manipulating statistics for political gain. Instead, his findings were greeted with the silence of assent—these facts are no longer a source of dispute.

There is an ongoing debate in conservative circles, however, about the nature of the solution to our problems. One camp argues for economic solutions, the other for social ones. In the economic camp, we hear the arguments—"What's really wrong with our country today is that people do not have jobs. If we can go into our urban areas and introduce enterprise zones then we could revitalize those areas, get people jobs, and turn this thing around." If, indeed, it is only a matter of economics and money, why are there so many rich criminals? If we take money and pour it into a community without fundamentally changing the culture of that community, all we will have is a lot of money floating around the still-existing problem. Jack Kemp recently said,

It is in families that children learn the tools of economic

success and moral restraint. This is why our economic life and our moral life are inseparable. Economics is more than a matter of interest rates and deficits. Morality is more than a matter of stained glass and hymns. Economic success is built on moral foundations. The strength of our values is the source of many other strengths.... Without moral convictions a society cannot thrive. Without moral convictions, its success would mean little.... We are concerned about values because a growing GNP is not the only measure of our greatness. What would it profit America to gain the whole world and lose our own children? What would it benefit our nation if we were rich in possessions and poor in ideals?

His synopsis of this debate is a prelude to the recognition that government is not the primary agent of change in our culture, that education is not the primary agent of change in our culture, that money, self-esteem, and opportunity are not the primary agents of change. If only they were. If only government could change things, how much easier our job would be.

During the 1980s we prospered economically under the leadership of Ronald Reagan. Our peacetime economic expansion was unrivaled in all of human history. Nevertheless, our moral crises grew. The 1980s saw the introduction of a new drug that decimated our inner cities, the introduction of Madonna's soft porn into everyday life ... If the answer had remained solely in the realm of government, I am convinced that things would have changed for the better; unfortunately they did not.

If the answer were simply money, why are the inner cities of today not doing better? Not only have they been the recipients of trillions of dollars in the past thirty years, but they are also the sites of a booming economy, albeit an illegal and underground one. Make no mistake about it—there is money in the inner cities, and that money has not helped civilize people.

We are a society of contradictions. We want and expect our government to solve our problems. We want and expect our government to be upright and moral. We are outraged when it is not, yet we also hold our politicians to little or no accountability in their personal lives.

We are shocked to read about atrocity after atrocity perpetrated by younger and younger people. Yet Michael Medved, Hollywood film critic, estimates that by the time the average child reaches age eighteen, he will have seen more than fifteen thousand murders on television or in the movies. We are shocked that as we tolerate violence in the popular culture, the young in our society are becoming increasingly violent.

A generation of children is being raised without men in their lives—more than seventy percent of all felons were raised without a father, as Michael Medved writes in *Hollywood vs. America*. Nevertheless, we are shocked when those same children who have not learned what it really means to be loved, become predators on our streets.

We hand out as many condoms as textbooks and treat young men and women as though they were animals in heat. We are shocked that we have raised a generation of children who engage in rampant promiscuity and record numbers of unmarried teens giving birth. And we will weep as more and more young and old die of AIDS.

We mock commitments and covenants—"it just feels right," . . . "just do it." We are shocked that America's divorce rate is the highest in the world and that fathers abandon their children and are never heard from again.

C. S. Lewis summarized these apparent contradictions well in *The Abolition of Man* when he wrote, "[W]e continue to clamor for those very qualities we are rendering impossible. We make men without chests and expect of them virtue and enterprise. We laugh at honor and are shocked to find traitors in our midst."

Our need is great. And I fear we are just beginning to reap the fruit of our bitter harvest. The violence and the desperation of today are really the result of the violence and desperation of the middle and late 1970s. The children, the young men and women of today who appear to be careening out of control, are not the children of 1995 but of 1980. They were raised on *Happy Days* and *Laverne and Shirley*. They listened to the music of Bobby Brown, Tears for Fears, Michael Jackson, and The Police. They lived through an era of economic growth for all classes. But still we see around us desperation, violence, hopelessness. Of the angry young men and women of today, about seven percent were born to parents out of wedlock.

Of the children and young adults of the years 2005 and 2010, about thirty percent will have been born out of wedlock. They will have grown up in a brave new world of "gangsta rap" artists like Snoop Doggy Dogg, Ice-T, grunge-scene bands like Nirvana, Pearl Jam, and the violent hard-core rock of Guns'n'-Roses. They play video games like "Mortal Combat" and watch shows like *NYPD Blue*. I fear for these children, and I fear for our future, because I think that we do not yet realize the horrors that we will witness *unless* we confront the fact that even if a village could raise a child, our national village could not *unless* we take the time to be individuals of character who care for those who need to be cared for; *unless* we take the time to be families that raise children who will be people of character; *unless* we turn our communities into communities and not collections of people sharing space; and *unless* we become a nation that values all of its citizens, great and small, born and unborn.

Sloughing off our responsibilities on government is easy. Rebuilding our village is not. If we want to reclaim our society, exactly what we need to do is to rebuild our village one institution at a time—not in some vain attempt to recapture the past and encase it in Plexiglas but rebuild a village that is striving and productive in our complex twentieth-century world. We have the skills and the tools. We *can* do it!

Chapter Three

Yes, We Can!

Were it not for a grandmother that she did not know, Ladeeta Smith's job working for drug dealers could well have been the last job of her life. Thanks to Thelma Simmons, it probably will not even have been the most lucrative.

When Ladeeta's mother was arrested for drug use, the sixty-six-year-old Mrs. Simmons took charge. Having already raised eight children of her own and still caring for a nineteen-year-old grandson, Thelma knew kids. She took in Ladeeta and her sisters because she knew that if they were to have a chance, it required her effort.

"I pray," Thelma says. "Otherwise, I would have cracked up a long time ago. It is a terrible thing to lose a child, but I [knew] I had to be there for these young ones coming up." Be there, she was.

Thelma moved Ladeeta to Crown Heights, Brooklyn where Ladeeta began to know that elusive thing called childhood. She also began to know something called hard work. She was admitted to the Boys & Girls High School, and there she met principal Frank Mickens. The enforcer with a strict dress code, a low tolerance for troublemakers, and a reputation for turning around "hopeless" students, Frank became Ladeeta's surrogate father and role model.

It was the love of Mrs. Simmons, the care of Mr. Mickens, the atmosphere of love and respect at Boys & Girls, and an inner strength *and courage that now has Ladeeta looking forward to college and a new life.*

In *Democracy in America*, Alexis de Tocqueville called our private institutions—families, churches, civic institutions, fellowships, and schools—the immune system of our nation. He said that these voluntary associations were our "values-generating institutions." Goodness, he wrote, does not exist in a vacuum but must be encouraged, upheld, and repeated by our most basic institutions. He warned that if they failed or if the government attempted to step in and fill that role, our nation would be in grave danger of decline and eventual collapse. It seems as though we took his words as a prescription rather than as a warning.

Looking back over my life, I see clearly that government programs and court decisions played a major role in my advancement, but I also see clearly that my faith, my family, and my community played an even greater role.

Were it not for the strength of my family and community, I would never have been able to take advantage of the governmental legislation that gave me greater freedom. If my mother, my aunt, my uncle, and the rest of my family had not taught me honesty, courage, faith, perseverance, and hope, my life would have been one destined for the back of the line and the back of the bus.

Were it not for schools that demanded that I learn not only how to read and write but also how to think, my life would have been one destined for frustration and bitterness. I would not only have lacked the basic skills needed to advance, I would also have known that I was not living up to what I *could* have been.

Were it not for churches that helped me set my mood

compass, understand and develop my growing faith, teach me right from wrong, and give me hope, my life would have been one destined for pregnancies out of wedlock, a string of ne'er-do-well boyfriends, and a fate of being old before my time.

Were it not for businesses that were forced to hire young blacks, my life would have been one destined for inferior work prospects, inferior self-esteem, and inferior opportunity. I would not have been able to meet my wonderful husband, raise three beautiful children, and be a productive participant in life.

If we want to reconstruct the village, we need to rebuild much more than our town hall. We need to build up the family, the church, the schools, the businesses, and neighborhoods. *We can transform America*. We did once before.

Children huddled in the streets. Families waited for food from the generous. Crime rates increased rapidly. One journalist calculated that if all of New York's liquor stores, gambling halls, and houses of prostitution were lined up on a single street, that street would extend for thirty miles. On that street there was a robbery every 165 yards, a murder every half mile, and thirty reporters offering sensational detail. That was New York in the late nineteenth century. Does it sound familiar? It should, because it is part of our history. Scholars have actually said that the problems faced in the 1870s and 1880s were problems worse than those that we confront today.

Clearly, things changed. But how? Things changed because individuals, families, churches, and civic organizations, motivated by a desire to help, mobilized. They knew that they had to put themselves on the line. They knew that compassion means *suffering with*, so they started organizations and took actions that they knew would really help. The helpless were helped. Truth and virtue were modeled. Sacrifices were made.

This process took decades, not weeks. That we must

remember. In my lifetime I have seen change that I could not have imagined, but it has been slow, and the advances have been incremental. We have the tendency to want change and to want it now. We need look no further than the anger displayed in the 1992 presidential elections. People were angry and did not want to give the "status quo" another minute of time. By the close of Bill Clinton's first year in office, only forty percent of people say that they would vote for Bill "the agent of change" Clinton a second time. Where Republicans were rejected en masse in 1992, today they control the United States Senate and have near-record numbers in the House. We should be impatient with violence, poverty, racism, injustice, a poor education system, unborn children being denied their right to life, and diseases with no cures. We should also recognize that real, lasting cultural change does not come about easily or quickly.

How long will this type of change take? The question is irrelevant. It does not matter how long it will take. It's not our concern. That is why we cannot be discouraged about where we are right now. We have a long road ahead of us. We may never live to see a Constitutional ban overturning *Roe v. Wade*, but does that mean that we stop fighting? No. We may never live to see the grandchildren of the children that we help today through our care and our concern, but does that mean that we stop caring? No. We may never live to see the day when the church is once again a beacon of light to a hurting world, not a flickering candle in the darkness. But does that mean that we stop believing? No. We may not see a cure for AIDS in our lifetime, but does that mean that we stop the research? No.

There is a tradition in our family. Every year we pile into the car with the kids and we go to the beach. When the children were young, invariably the same question would be asked even before we left the driveway— "How long till we get there?"

Typically on these trips, Charles and I do not talk until two hours into the trip because of the stress of getting everything in order. But upon hearing that question, Charles will turn with clenched teeth and say to Chuck, "Do you want to go to the beach?" Chuck responds with, "Yes . . ." Charles then trumps him, saying, "Then it doesn't matter how long it takes to get there."

If we want to have an impact on the world, then it really does not matter how long it will take to get there. As much as we care about this journey, we must recognize that we may never see it to completion.

Changing our culture requires changed outlooks. Our cultural renewal agenda must be an agenda not only of voter registration but of character checks; not only of direct mail but of directed families; not only of strong opposition research but of strong community involvement; and not only a national turn-out-the-vote drive but a national conviction of the need for cultural change.

If you still question this premise, consider for a moment the debate of the day: health care. As this book is being written, Democrats and Republicans are scrambling to come up with the best reforms to ensure universal access, quality care, affordability, and doctor choice. But none of these proposals will amount to a hill of beans if we do not change our behavior. We have this attitude in our country: We want to eat all we want to eat, drink all we want to drink, smoke whatever we want to smoke, have whatever kind of sexual relationships we want to avoid, exercise, ignor seatbelts, not get sick or hurt or injured, and then demand that the government provide health care and fix us so that we can then repeat our irresponsible behaviors.

The reality is, if people continue to smoke, continue to be couch potatoes, continue to eat junk food, and continue in habits of alcohol and drug abuse, the best health-care system in the world cannot save them and the richest nation in the world cannot afford to pay for it. The American Medical Association recently estimated that the health care costs of "unhealthy habits" are $171 billion a year, or more than twenty percent of our national health care bill. Substance abuse of drugs, tobacco, and alcohol costs society between $140 billion and $238 billion a year, figures that exclude the costs of treatment for diseases exacerbated but not caused by substance abuse. In 1990, the cost of just three sexually transmitted diseases (STDs) was $5.4 billion. If we factor in other behavior-driven social pathologies such as AIDS, violence, and illegitimate births, these figures are much higher.

In my experience, in the struggle to rebuild the village there are two camps of people that I tend to encounter in Washington. First, there are those who believe that the political answers are the only answers, because they have a fundamental belief that you cannot change the culture. This group of people crosses all ideological, political, and racial boundaries. Those on its left tend to be people who fundamentally believe you cannot change the culture; therefore, we might as well adopt policies and programs that deal with "reality" where we are. They have given up and said, "Let's just deal with today." Unfortunately, there are a growing number of "conservatives" who believe the same thing. They usually manifest themselves by saying that the culture is rotten, that there is no hope for its improvement, so let's retreat into our churches and into our families. This group solely prays, because they believe that nothing else can be done. Both of these camps are wrong.

The first thing we need to do is to define the problem. Once we have done that, we can develop a strategic plan and implement it. On top of a right understanding of the issues, however, we must live the Gospel as a people, love as a family, unite as a community, and demand justice as a nation. This is a call for nothing less than laying down our lives in love.

Conservatives are known for being advocates of personal responsibility. We advocate it in our welfare reform proposals: no welfare if you do not work. We advocate it in our criminal reform proposals: If you commit a crime, you will go to jail. Unfortunately, we have not advocated it enough. Or, perhaps we have just not *lived* it enough.

Recently, it seems that both liberals *and* conservatives have been debating little else besides the reconstruction and expansion of the town hall in our mythical village. Do not get me wrong—government does many things well. It can use its vast resources to ensure the safety of our food and the stability of our currency. It can create legislation that gives freedom to the captive. But government cannot tell a child when to go to bed at night. Government cannot tuck a child in and bestow a hug. Government cannot motivate me to get out of bed in the morning, shower, put on my clothes, and go to work. Government cannot cook my dinner, wash my children's clothes, or put Band-Aids on their knees. And government certainly cannot teach my children right from wrong. But all of these things need to be done—first by the individual, then by the family and the community. That will change our land.

I have been told, and I have read and seen no evidence to the contrary, that every great cultural change in this country was preceded by a spiritual reawakening. It was true of the efforts to grant civil rights to black Americans. It is no accident that Martin Luther King, Jr. was first and foremost a preacher of the Word of God. In a sermon he preached in Montgomery, Alabama, in 1956, he said, "I still believe that standing up for the truth of God is the greatest thing in the world. This is the end of life. The end of life is not to be happy. The end of life is not to achieve pleasure and avoid pain. The end of life is to do the will of God, come what may."

If you picked up this book, thinking that it would offer some ingenious new policy prescriptions, be advised: It does not. It is true that it is a "how-to" book about cultural renewal. Yet my answers are not new. In fact, they are quite old.

Chapter Four

Individuals

Not far from my home in Virginia lies the city of Alexandria, a beautiful and historic old city founded before America was a nation. It has seen our country in times of war and times of triumph, times of turmoil and times of peace. Like the rest of the nation, it has recently seen an outburst in youth violence. In 1987, twenty-one juveniles there were accused of killing people. In 1992, the number had increased to sixty-two. Arrests for juvenile assault have risen ninety-seven percent in the last decade. Among the cases: an eleven-year-old who is afraid to go to school because other girls have threatened her. A thirteen-year-old who took a starter's pistol to school after a skirmish between two groups. Another thirteen-year-old who stuffed a rock inside a sock and clobbered a classmate. A seven-year-old girl who said another seven-year-old girl threatened to kill her if she did not turn over her mother's jewelry.

It was into this cauldron that Alexandria Detective Dana Lawhorne was called. His is another story of how one individual's commitment so profoundly has an impact on those around him. Burdened with a caseload exceeding two hundred cases, he is intimately involved in the lives of those on whom he has made an impact. He believes that early police involvement in the youth community teaches teenagers that their actions have consequences. In less serious cases, likely to the chagrin of "tougher" cops around him, he has some discretion in filing charges. He knows the youth, and he bases his decisions on the seriousness of the offense, the individual's history, and whether the victim wants to prosecute. He spends time in the children's homes, he looks at their performance in school, their character, and their parents. For one youthful offender, psychological counseling might be in order. For another, he assigns community service or restitution.

Dana Lawhorne could have been promoted long ago. He could have moved on to a higher paying job, one that does not require him to drive around a city looking for signs of problems—for graffiti marking the signs of gangs, for armed youths in a knife fight, for hopeless-feeling girls and angry young men who want to lash out. But Dana Lawhorne has forgone promotion and stuck with this lower-paying position because he believes he is doing what is right. He is. The impact that his life has had on the youth who know him cannot be quantified. Neither can it be written into law. I am sure his decision to stay was not an easy one. I am also sure that his sacrifice is something we must emulate.

We should not fall prey to the doom and gloom outlook that is so pervasive today. We should have an expanded worldview. *We must be moved to the service of God and to the service of man.*

But this is not a fight in which to engage on your own. This fight is brutal, and without a strong community of support, the culture will devour you. Without a spiritual home, this culture will devour you. As this book is being completed, I am in the process of changing jobs. Newly elected Virginia Governor George Allen has appointed me as his Secretary for Health and Human Resources. The job will be difficult, as will be the opposition. I am undertaking this task because I believe I can make a difference in the lives of Virginians and because I believe that God has called me to public service. In this process, it is amazing to me that there are people who have said, "We will find housing options for you." Others have said, "We will pray for you, care for your children, prepare your meals." That kind of support plays a very real role in my life, and I do not know how we can engage the culture without that practical, loving support that allows us to keep going.

I believe that change in our country will only happen as change happens in individuals—from the inside out and from the bottom up. What are some things we can do? We should try:

- volunteering in an AIDS hospice
- adopting a special-needs child
- providing shelter to a woman in a crisis pregnancy
- donating ten percent of our time to work with children in the inner city
- encouraging churches to open their doors to homeless people
- teaching in Sunday school

It is tough. And we cannot do it alone. James Baldwin wrote, "I think you owe it to me, as my friend, to fight me, to let me get away with nothing, to force me to be clear, to force me to be honest, allow me to take no refuge in rage or in despair and of course, I owe you the same. This means that we are certainly going to hurt each other's feelings from time to time. But that is one of the ways in which people learn from each other." Imagine for a moment what our homes, what our communities, and what our nation would look like if we all were to pay the price of true friendship. If just one out of every four adults mentored a child, imagine for a moment what that would mean to a generation of children who do not know that anyone loves them.

Imagine for a moment what our homes, what our communities, and what our nation would look like if every member of our churches were to spend ten percent of their time working with children, working with the elderly, working with the blind, the handicapped, the college student.... Imagine.

Individual commitment is where it all begins. If there is no commitment, then this is where it all ends. Put away this book, because it will just be an intellectual exercise that will not do anyone any good.

In June 1965 in Cape Town, South Africa, a lone man ascended the stairs to the rostrum and began to speak. He knew that his words that night would be scrutinized and his meanings twisted. Yet he also knew there was a message that he felt compelled to deliver. It was not a popular message; in fact, it was a message that could have begun a riot or led to his death. Yet he spoke haltingly as he began, uncertain of the crowd, uncertain of his delivery. His passion rose with the intensity of the address, however, and toward the end of the speech he said,

> It is from numberless diverse acts of courage and belief that human history is shaped. Each time a man stands up for an ideal, or acts to improve the lot of others, or strikes out against injustice, he sends forth a tiny ripple of hope, and crossing each other from a million different centers of energy and daring those ripples build a current which can sweep down the mightiest walls of oppression and resistance.

He went on to discuss the other dangers: expediency and timidity. When he was through, Robert Kennedy walked through the all-white audience in Cape Town, South Africa, to meet with those who were not allowed to hear his address.

His call is one we need to heed today. Our call is not a call to some unattainable utopia. It is not to create a heaven here on earth—that can never happen. It is a call to fulfill Christ's commission to His people—to care for His flock, to serve our neighbor. To ignore that part of Christ's message is to compromise His Incarnation. We must each endeavor to undertake this task and do it for His glory. It is costly: emotionally, physically, financially, and spiritually.

Do you want to know how to transform America? Look in the mirror. Look to God. Fall to your knees. Ask Him to change you. Get up. Live life. As long as we can keep the problems at arm's length, we can keep the solutions there as well. It is easy to demand change in our government, change in our economic system, and change in our social institution—but to transform America, *we* must be a *changed* people.

Chapter Five

Families

*No matter how many communes anybody invents,
the family always creeps back.*

—MARGARET MEAD

He had always excelled. School was easy. He was good at sports. He was popular. He was student head of the Sunday school class. Why should his parents worry about him? Occasionally, he would play his music too loudly. Occasionally, a curse word would jump out when he was really angry, and the parties that he went to on weekends often left him smelling like alcohol and cigarettes. But he was never drunk. And he assured them that he was never the one smoking. They knew all too well how easily tobacco smoke permeated clothing and makes you stink.

He had been dating the same girl for years. They had met in the sixth grade and had spent hours together. His mother loved seeing them come home from school together. They would make a beeline for his room—ever since the sixth grade. She thought back to the days when she would bring them refreshments, only to find them engaged in an exciting board game or video game.

But as time went by and she got busier and busier with the younger children, she had less and less time to monitor them. She *figured that they got by okay. She always made sure that there were plenty of nutritious juices in the refrigerator, and she always made sure that there was plenty of fruit on the counter. Both were athletic, and sometimes when she would come home from work, she would hear one of them in the shower.* Always exercising, *she thought with a smile.*

Her husband had his own thoughts—of pride. As a deacon in the church he frequently heard about the trials and tribulations of other families, other godly families. But he knew his children. They were good kids. He thought back to his own childhood ... Going out with the guys to the drug store to the ice-cream fountain ... Meeting some girls and talking with them over hamburgers. He was so glad that his son was having as much fun as he was.

The phone rang late one night. She rolled over and picked it up. His party got closed down by the police, and he needed a ride. Ah, the joys of parenting! She got in the car and drove to Chris's house. As she pulled around the corner, her eyes were assaulted with the wailing of sirens and a row of brake lights.

He stumbled into the car. The smell of alcohol was worse this time, and it seemed to be coming from his breath, not his clothes. He was drunk, and judging from the other kids staggering out of the house, they were also. Not much was said as they drove home.

The next day the story started to come out. Frantic phone calls were made by parents shocked that their kids had been drunk. Phone calls were received from the dean of the Christian school, and it became clear very quickly that this was going to be a big scandal.

The parents quickly mobilized behind their kids. The students stood steadfast in their stories that this was just one party that got out of hand. But as time passed, that, too, proved to be a lie. That particular party at Chris's house took place when his parents were out of town. The party was almost exclusively attended by kids from the Christian school, and the details were sordid: sex in the hot tub, drug paraphernalia found in the house, three kegs of beer, not a single student over the age of seventeen. The school officials maintained that this was not an isolated incident, and soon, many of the students from the party admitted the same thing.

Their son, the school maintained, was one of the ringleaders. Other students looked to him as the one who could "be a Christian and still be cool." Testimony revealed that he and Ann had been having sex since the seventh grade. She had already had an abortion, as had some of the other girls.

The parents did not believe it was true. Not my child!

Just how important is the family to society? Let's start with the first family—no, not the President and his family—Adam and Eve. Have you ever stopped to think about them? No, not just about the "forbidden fruit" but about the repercussions of one messed-up family?

When Adam sinned, not only did it interfere with his relationship with his wife, but murder entered the human scene because Cain killed Abel. Immorality entered the human scene because polygamy came about. So that by the time we get to Genesis 6, the whole world has been destroyed. All because one family was so dysfunctional.

As we look out across this nation, what kind of children are we raising? Are we raising children of virtue? Are we raising children who can weather the tough storms? Are we raising children to whom others will look to as leaders, husbands, and wives?

In his new book, *Right from Wrong*, Josh McDowell reveals that among "Christian" youth, two-thirds regularly lied, nearly forty percent cheated on exams, ten percent used illegal drugs, and more than half had been sexually intimate with another person. McDowell said, "It is painfully apparent that many of our own youth have lost the ability to distinguish right from wrong. Many no longer pursue their parents' dreams and values but instead absorb the warped values of a sick society."

The reality is that although we profess to believe certain things and certain ways of living, we are not translating them to our children. If we want to affect the culture, we must be raising kids differently, which can only happen if we are committed to creating the best environments for children to grow and flourish in—strong families.

The very people we count on to raise strong and vibrant children are not always doing it. Of course, there are children who will rebel no matter the quality and strength of parenting. And of course, there are children who will thrive and excel despite having faced more hardships than any child should have to endure. Nevertheless, as we examine ourselves, and as we examine our families, I believe that we need to *be* more and we need to *do* more.

A couple of years ago, Charles and I received an invitation to go to the Soviet Union to talk about families. The invitation was a surprise, but what we found when we got there was even more remarkable. I expected cool stares, detached conversations, and disinterested people. I found people who had been through years of familial destruction and moral disintegration. I discovered the aftermath of an Orwellian state, a state that tried to control thought, speech, and emotion—a state crumbling under the unbreakable tenacity of the human spirit.

The Russian bureaucrats' profound appreciation and interest in the family stood in stark contrast to the Bush-Quayle '92 campaign that I had left for a couple of weeks. They realized that before they could build a strong economy, they had to have strong families. They realized that before they could see a powerful currency, they had to have strong families. They realized that before they could see entrepreneurial expansion, they had to have strong families. They realized, in short, that what mattered most was not "the economy, stupid." One man said to me, "Our economic system will not work in the future, if, as we have learned from our past, our people are not honest, strong, and good. Unless we change our present course, we will fail in our social and economic reforms, and the world will fail with us." He went on to say, "Contracts will mean nothing unless people honor them. The education system will not work unless people value education and love the children they teach. The military will not work unless people understand honor and sacrificial love of country. There is only one place," he said, "where such values can be taught: the family. I know," he said, "because for nearly two-thirds of my life I have tried to instill those values through the State and through the government, through order and through law, and I have failed, and we have failed."

That Russian bureaucrat understood something that late September day that more and more people are beginning to understand today. As President Lyndon Johnson said in a commencement address at Howard University in 1965, "The family is the cornerstone of our society. More than any other force it shapes the attitudes, the hopes, the ambitions, and the values of the child. And when the family collapses, it is the children that are usually damaged. When it happens on a massive scale, the community itself is crippled."

The evidence is completely overwhelming. One would have to be intellectually dishonest not to recognize it. All sides of the political spectrum now acknowledge it. Bill Galston is a domestic policy adviser to Bill Clinton. Not too long ago he wrote in *Mandate for Change*, "The economic consequences of a parent's absence are often accompanied by psychological consequences, which include higher than average levels of youth suicide, low intellectual and educational performance, and higher than average rates of mental illness, violence, and drug use." This recognition by all sides of the political debate, however, will be all for naught if parents do not live up to their responsibilities as parents.

I have heard it said time and again that the state requires a person to have a license to own a dog, but anyone can have a child. Parenthood, having and raising children, is an awesome, awesome, responsibility. Children come into this world *completely* dependent. They do not know how to feed themselves, protect themselves, or care for themselves. They *need* so many things. Then they become teenagers. . . .

. . . And need even more. Their needs may not be as apparent as changing diapers and cleaning up messes, but they are just as important. Several years ago, Chuck, my "baby," was preparing to go to college. As he prepared to leave home for the first time, I was filled with a deep sense of joy and anxiety. Had I done all that I could to instill in him the values that would carry him through life? Had I taught him about the importance of honesty, compassion, faith, love, friendship, loyalty, courage, and perseverance? I feared that I had not . . . so I spent his last few days at home trying to cover everything from how to sort laundry to what it means to be a person of character. "Chuck," I said, "Have I taught you about honesty? Have I taught you about the importance of keeping your word? Have I told you about the time that your grandmother—?" The last few days rushed by as we talked. But the more I talked, the more I realized that my parenting with Chuck had changed. He had lived in our home for eighteen years. He *knew* me. He *knew* Charles. If we were the kind of people we wanted him to be, if we had lived what we had taught, Chuck would know that by now. If we had not, no amount of badgering could change what we had been.

One of the reasons that Chuck *knew* our rules, our standards, and our values was that Chuck had experienced them firsthand. *You cannot instill in a few days what takes a lifetime to build into a child.*

During my years at the National Right to Life Committee, glamorous black-tie gatherings were the exception, definitely not the rule. One of the things I most looked forward to every year was a fancy party, held on a yacht circling around Manhattan island. It was the highlight of my year. The Archbishop of New York was there, many celebrities were there, and *I* was there. This particular year I was even more excited than usual to go—just ask Charles. I had gone out and bought a new dress. I had my hair done. I had my nails done. Heck, I even had my toenails done. As I was admiring my dress and my locks yet another time, the phone rang. On the other end was the principal of the school that our youngest child, Robbie, attended.

The principal's voice had that sound that only disappointed and angry parents or guardians have. It seems that during a particular morning activity, Robbie decided that he was tired of participating and wanted to stop. When other students and the teacher told him that "everyone" meant *everyone*, Robbie put forth a colorful colloquy of words that his dear teacher found quite inappropriate for a nine-year-old child, or any child of any age, for that matter. Young Robert was promptly marched down to the principal's office and forced to sit for an extended period of time, contemplating his indiscretion.

Upon hearing this little tale, I became angry and disappointed. After all, here was *my* child behaving in a manner differing little from the behavior of the children we had raised him *not* to copy. I was determined to make an impression.

Charles was, too. He canceled the trip. "Kay, we have got to nip this thing in the bud," he said. I did not buy it.

It is 3:30, and I'm angry because we should be in New York and I should be getting ready to put on my new dress. Instead, it's hanging in the closet, and I am watching Robbie getting off the bus, dragging his knapsack up the walk—the embodiment of fear.

Breaking in on my pouting, Charles said to me, "If we got a call from school informing us that Robbie had broken his leg, we would have immediately canceled the trip and rushed out to the hospital to be with him as they set the bone. Well," he said, "we have just received a phone call telling us that our son has a break in his character. We will now set *that*, because it is much more important."

Robbie finally made it into the house, and we were waiting for him. Charles was extraordinary. He asked Robbie, "Why do you think we are here?" Robbie responded, "Because I did something bad." "No," Charles said, "not because you *did* something bad. We are here because we love you. And because we love you, we care enough to point out to you the flaw in your character. And because we love you, we care enough to set it straight." He went on to explain to Robbie what he had so painstakingly explained to me earlier. This break in his character was more important than a break in any limb. He talked to Robbie about who we are as a people, as a family, and as individuals. He took more than an hour to work with Robbie in helping him understand all these things.

Finally, Charles said, "Part of the problem is that your mind is not filled with the proper things. Your mind is filled with things that do not edify, that do not inspire, and that do not instill goodness. Therefore, you will be grounded until you memorize and meditate on the Apostles' Creed, the Twenty-third Psalm, and the Lord's Prayer."

I cannot recall a time when I was prouder of my husband. The work of shaping character is hard work, time-consuming work, painful work. One of the stupidest things I have ever heard is the debate over "quantity" versus "quality" time. To think that you can have quality without quantity is to ignore one of the most fundamental realities of family life. It oftentimes takes hours to just start to get to the root of the problem. Then it takes several more hours or days to work on solving the problem.

I have found some of the best conversations have been not in the first ten, fifteen, or thirty minutes but in the several hours that follow. We cannot simply say that we will spend thirty quality minutes with a child per day. It will not work. Parenting means loving your child, setting character flaws straight, and spending a great portion of time with them. What does it mean specifically? It may mean delaying a staff meeting because something comes up that must be dealt with right away. It may mean sitting at the table for an hour and a half sorting it out, using it as an opportunity to teach and retrain. It is exhausting and time-consuming, and not just for the kids. However, it makes us, as parents, better people.

During the 1992 presidential campaign, Vice-President Dan Quayle was vigorously attacked by many conservatives because of what he said on *Larry King Live!*—that he would support and love his daughter if she came to him and said that she had had an abortion. The vice-president was attacked because, many said, he was being hypocritical in his pro-life position. What Dan Quayle said was what any loving parent should have said. If *we* do not love our children unconditionally, who do we think *will?*

If we think that we can allow children to fend for themselves, if we think that our actions have little influence and our language has much, if we think we can just dabble in family, we will have doomed ourselves to creating a generation of children incapable of being parents, incapable of being trustworthy, incapable of being the people of virtue that this nation needs so desperately.

Late that evening, when I should have been schmoozing on the yacht, I heard a chorus of little voices saying, "Surely, goodness and mercy will follow me every day of my life and I shall dwell in the house of the Lord forever." As I looked around the room, Bizzie and Chuck were standing behind Robbie, encouraging him and helping him with the memorization verses. Charles's "punishment" had turned into a time for the family to come together. Chuck and Bizzie had stayed up with their brother, memorizing the verses, talking about the meaning of the verses, and talking about the importance of living as people of honor. "I believe in God the Father Almighty, the maker of heaven, the maker of earth . . ." Such is the work of the family. Such is the surest formula for renewal as a nation that I know.

Chapter Six

The Community

*Individual liberty is individual power, and as the power of a community
is a mass compounded of individual powers, the nation which enjoys
the most freedom must necessarily be in proportion
to its numbers the most powerful nation.*

—John Quincy Adams

*The demonstrators were parents. They came from their homes
and their places of work. They were mainly black and Latino. Their
signs were homemade, but one way and another, their awkwardly
lettered signs all said the same thing—that these parents were in a
furor over an educational system that proposed to hand out condoms
to schoolchildren.*

*A black minister, and the father of two young children stepped
forward saying, "If you want the right to train children, you first had
better take care of them when they're sick, sit up with them all night,
hold them, comfort them, clothe and feed them."*

Yet another said, "We will win, and we will not end here."

*The proposal was withdrawn, and the parents did not with-
draw—they engaged.*

*Months later, in Queens, a feisty widow grandmother named
Mary Cummins, who also happens to chair a local school board,*

confronted New York City Schools' Chancellor Joseph Fernandez and the city's education bureaucracy about the "Children of the Rainbow" curriculum, which calls for first graders to be taught about homosexuality as "just another lifestyle."

Vilified by the left and by the media as a bigot, Mrs. Cummins refused to compromise on what she viewed as an issue of principle. "I would never give up on a principle. I'd go out and scrub floors before I give up on a principle. I found out that wars are lost because people are not persistent. You have to be persistent. . . . These are our kids."

Her tough stand created a chain reaction as other school boards across the city began to realize that they, too, could resist the effort to impose political correctness in the first-grade classroom. An all-black school board became the second to say no to "Children of the Rainbow." And then there was another. And another.

The New York City education establishment went after Cummins with all of the force they could muster. The entire board was suspended. Fernandez called Mary Cummins "out of touch."

Several months later, after his own board turned against him, the Chancellor was out of a job, the "Children of the Rainbow" curriculum was dead, and an entire community was engaged and changed. Mary Cummins went back to her life as a grandmother and as chair of Queens, New York School Board #24.

In the quest to rebuild our common village, community institutions are vital. Whether they are loose confederations of individuals or families gathered together for a common purpose, or whether they are simply a neighborhood that unites against crime, the power of the community cannot be denied.

It is, after all, the broader community that enforces or contradicts the family's teachings and each individual's morality. As such, businesses, churches, schools and universities, the arts, and other civic institutions must be examined and strengthened. And the loose groupings of people along ethnic or racial lines are vital to strengthening our culture as well.

All across the United States, there are stories about communities like that little neighborhood in Queens, New York, that decided it was fed up with the way things were going and decided to make a change. There is a community in inner-city Chicago that fought back against violent crime and *won*. There is a community in inner-city Washington, D.C., that reclaimed a park that had been commandeered by drug pushers and winos. There is a community of businessmen in Los Angeles who are getting together to impose financial accountability for their corporate donations. There is a community of artists in Dallas that is promoting lifestyles that will not end in disease or destruction but in vitality and joy. These are the success stories. These are the communities that we need to emulate.

The parents who marched on New York City Hall that day decided that they were not prepared to sit back and allow the schools to fundamentally define the moral and sexual education of their children. They decided to band together to make a change. Who were these people? Who made up this community? They were people from all walks of life. There were doctors, lawyers, homemakers, nannies, cab drivers, garment workers, students, and businessmen, to name just a few. They were also people from all faiths. The signs that bespoke their opposition to the chancellor and his curriculum said, "Christians Say No," "Muslims Say No," and "Jews Say No."

The community in Washington that reclaimed its park from drug dealers did not have any millionaires. It did not have any star athletes. It did not have any movie stars. It had no celebrities at all. What it did have, however, was a group of individuals who shared a common goal and a common vision and who took the time to care. And you know what? I believe that if you looked in on their families, you would see families that reflected these individuals' love and commitment. I also believe that if you polled all of those people in New York, there would be just as many areas of *disagreement* in their views on issues as there were areas of *agreement.* The secret here is that these people put aside their differences to affect change in an area of common concern. Note the difference that they made.

When I was working in the White House Drug Office, one of the requirements for our involvement in drug intervention was community participation. It was accepted without question that if we were to really make a difference in a particular locale, it would only be with *full* community cooperation. So crucial was this kind of involvement that they would not be eligible for federal grants unless they brought in a broad-based team of community representatives all of whom pledged to be involved.

It seems that the key to making this happen in the lives of *our* communities is a slight change in outlook. Instead of emphasizing differences, let us find the common ground in our common life. I know that this is not rocket science, but I also know that this idea is not "taking off around us," if you will excuse the pun.

Think of a person or a group in your community with whom you just fundamentally disagree. Is it a neighbor who voted for Bill Clinton? Is it a neighbor who voted for George Bush? Is it that group picketing at the abortion clinic on Saturday morning? Is it the ACLU? Now, think about the five things in life that are most important to you. I will bet you that with those individuals or with those groups you will share a common ground on *at least* two of those issues. Work with them.

I was in a meeting not too long ago with a representative

of a *very liberal* group. This group has espoused everything from quotas to nationalized health care, but on a particular part of welfare reform we found common ground. We will be working together on that issue. We will bring our assets and ideas; they will bring theirs. But together we will accomplish much.

The same should be true of our communities. There is too much that unites us in opposition to allow ourselves to be separated by differences. Step back for a moment and think about the parents in New York whose unity knocked down the mightiest obstacle: the New York City School System. Racially, politically, culturally, economically, and religiously diverse, they united. The same can be true of us.

Think for a moment about the tremendous needs of the black community. With homicide the leading cause of death for our young men, with illegitimacy rates approaching seventy-five percent of all births, and with a helpless, hopeless rage festering not too far beneath the surface, it is a community in dire need. Yet, there is a debate raging in the black community about what makes one "black." There are those who argue that to be black, you must live in the inner city, work in the inner city, and draw most of your meaning from the inner city. These people assert that *that* and *only* that is the black community. They assert that those who have left the inner city, moved to suburbia, and entered the professional class, have left the black community.

At a time of such desperate need, why have we chosen to divide ourselves along these lines? When a young, black urban child has no recognition of history, no ability to read, write, or even think, what does it matter if the person helping him is a black person from Harlem or Hoboken? At a time when strong, black role models are needed, what does it matter if they come from Newark or Newport? Who better than an African-American mentor can help these children?

The black community is not geographic. The black community is the nexus of those people who have shared the black experience. I believe it to be true that because of what we have faced as a people, there is a bond that holds us together. It does not matter if we are janitors, teachers, lawyers, doctors, athletes, bureaucrats, professors, or university presidents. It does not matter if we live in urban or suburban areas, we are all a part of the black community, bound by history, bound by tradition, bound by a common experience, and having certain rights, privileges and responsibilities associated with being a member of that community. It is *not* geographic.

What, finally, does this mean for us? Does it mean that we have to mobilize our community against drugs and crime and violence? Well, if that is a problem where we live, perhaps we should. Does it mean that we have to go down to the local crisis-pregnancy center and volunteer in that community of people? Well, if we feel called to go there, perhaps we should.

But ultimately, it means paying just a little more attention to your world. No matter where you live, you are in a geographic community. There are people who live in front of you, behind you, next to you, and maybe even above and below you. Get to know these people. Get to know their needs.

I remember hearing a story about a young family that was transferred to a new city. Day after day, the young mother sat at home with her children as the father worked long hours in an attempt to get established. One day in sheer frustration, she opened the door to her apartment, mixed up some brownies, put them in the oven, and said a prayer. Aided by the "have a free brownie, meet a new neighbor" sign posted on her door, people stopped by. By the time her husband arrived home late that night, this young mother had befriended not only a number of other lonely young mothers but a number of older men and women. That relationship grew, and from it sprang a caring community where the old helped the young in raising the youngest. No constitutional amendment arose, no bill was passed in Congress, no press was alerted, but a community was reinvigorated, knowledge was shared, fellowship was enjoyed. And a vital part of the village was renewed.

We need to make a coordinated effort, a full-court press, to bring our communities together to transform our culture. Our areas of agreement are many. The benefits will be mutual. We want to see drugs, violence, teenage pregnancies and poverty reduced; unborn children have a right to life; racism eliminated; and character and integrity restored. Let us work toward those goals.

With the advent of technology, the traditional notion of community has declined. Fewer and fewer of us spend weekends with our neighbors or even know our neighbors' names. But technological advancement allows us to gather together with other communities, communities of like-minded individuals.

While watching Steven Spielberg's remarkable film *Schindler's List,* I was struck by the power of communities. In his epic movie he reveals the transforming power of a group of different people with a common heritage thrown together mercilessly but surviving *together.* It also shows the ability of a single business community to actually save lives. It also offers us a warning. The Jewish community was brought together under adverse conditions, yet it pulled together and was able to save many. We stand at a point where we can go one of two ways: restoration or chaos. The choice is ours.

Not too long ago, upon meeting a stranger, people would ask, "What community do you live in?" The answer would be, "Well, I live in Burgundy Village," or "I live in the Hoffmann Lane community." Today the answer is more like, "I live on

Tremont Drive." There is a world of difference between the two. *The state of our communities is a good measure of the state of our society.* Two of the most important "community elements," churches and schools, will be discussed in the next two chapters.

Chapter Seven

Churches

While the church may seem to be experiencing a season of growth and prosperity, it is failing to move people to commitment and sacrifice. The hard truth is that we have substituted an institutionalized religion for the life-changing dynamic of a living faith. . . .When compared with previous generations of believers, we seem among the most thoroughly at peace with our culture, the least adept at transforming society, and the most desperate for a meaningful faith. Our raison d'être *is confused, our mission obscured, and our existence as a people in jeopardy.*

—CHARLES COLSON

". . . that saved a wretch like me./I once was lost but now am found,/Was blind, but now I see. . . ." The old hymn hung in the air as the pastor looked expectantly at the crowd. "If you feel lost today, know that there is an answer. If you feel like you need a church home today, know that this one is open. If you feel like you just need some-one to talk to today, I will be standing here in the front as we sing the final stanza to this hymn."

Oh, how he loved his church. He had been the senior pastor for nearly twenty years. As the congregation sang their last "Amen," he felt a certain satisfaction. He had come far. When he was growing up as a boy, nobody would have guessed that he would become a pastor.

But the call was clear. As was the heart that wanted to serve God. That seemed a long way off now, though he was happy to be here.

The sanctuary was beautiful. It had clear glass windows on the sides shaded by the great leaves of those old maples, a fine crimson carpet, and remarkable old mahogany pews. The old place kept its homey feel even after the nearly five hundred thousand dollar upgrade to it, the sound system, the organ, and the Sunday school facilities. It was nice to be able to worship in a place so nice.

People were smiling as they filed out. Some would head off to brunch. Some of the guys were getting together to play football near their homes. Still others needed to head to the mall to catch up on some shopping, and others to catch up on some office work. It was the same every Sunday; he took a certain satisfaction in that.

Turning around, he saw some kids running around the sanctuary and the deacons in the back office, counting the tithes. He was sure that they would run a deficit again this Sunday. Why, he wondered, don't people give anymore? Why, *he wondered,* aren't more people visiting the church? *They had moved this church to this area for a reason, but that reason seemed vague and hazy now. Had they overreached? Maybe they had just moved to make themselves feel better. He did not know.*

He was the last one left. It was about 2:00 P.M., and he had one last look around. He went back to the office and punched in the code... "C ... H ... R ... I ... S ... T ..." *He was greeted with the comforting:* Beep, Beep, Beep *of the countdown as the LCD flashed 60, 59, 58, 57.... He needed to hurry to get out of the church. He always thought it would be funny if he were the one that tripped the alarm. He could just see the cops pulling up with their guns drawn and ordering him to come out of the door with his hands up.*

Not this time. He hustled out the door, giving the lock a quarter turn before he left. The door slammed shut behind him, and he gave the knob a turn. It was locked. He pulled the key out of his pocket and flipped the deadbolt.

He walked to his car behind the chain-link fence, pulled out, locked the fence, and drove off. He never thought about classrooms to teach the young, kitchens that could feed the hungry, warmth that could comfort the homeless, the empty fellowship hall that could provide activities for the restless teens, or the unused church buses that could have provided transportation for the elderly.

There is an argument to be made that, person for person, today's church is one of the most irrelevant institutions in society. For all of the venom and fear spewed at members of the "religious right," most of today's churches are left alone. They not only do not stir up any anger, they do not rock the boat; in fact, most people are comfortable with them. Even the nonreligious tend to look at our churches as benign institutions that create a placid and docile citizenry, having little impact on our culture.

This was *not* the historical role of the church in America. Despite the fact that there has been so much debate in America about the proper role of church and state, our history is really quite clear. Far from erecting a wall to separate religion and public life, the First Amendment was intended to mean freedom *of* religion, not freedom *from* religion. Even Jefferson's now unpraiseworthy quote about the "wall of separation" was derived from a speech by Baptist preacher Roger Williams who advocated a "wall of separation" to protect the "garden of the church" from the "wilderness of the world."

Consider as well some of the following quotes by our nation's founders:

Of all the dispositions and habits which lead to political prosperity, religion and morality are indispensable supports. . . . The mere politician, equally with the pious man, ought to respect and to cherish them. . . . Whatever may be conceded to the influence of refined education . . . reason and experience both forbid us to expect that national morality can prevail in exclusion of a religious people.
—GEORGE WASHINGTON

Statesmen . . . may plan and speculate for liberty, but it is religion and morality alone, which can establish the principles upon which freedom can securely stand. The only foundation of a free constitution is pure virtue.
—JOHN ADAMS

And can liberties of a nation be thought secure when we have removed their only firm basis, a conviction in the minds of the people that these liberties are a gift of God? That they are not to be violated but with His wrath? Indeed I tremble for my country when I reflect that God is just; that his justice cannot sleep forever.
—THOMAS JEFFERSON
(*THE MYTH OF SEPARATION*, BY DAVID BURTON)

Consider where our country is today. According to several Supreme Court cases, a verbal prayer offered in a school is unconstitutional, even if it is both voluntary and denominationally neutral. Freedom of speech and the press is guaranteed to students unless the topic is religious, at which time such speech becomes unconstitutional. It is unconstitutional for a student to pray aloud over his lunch. It is unconstitutional for a war memorial to be erected in the design of a cross. It is unconstitutional for students to arrive at school early to hear a student volunteer read prayers that had been offered by the chaplains in the chambers of the U.S. Congress (See *State Board of Education v. Board of Education of Netcong*, 1970).

How has this happened? We are a nation of churchgoers—by far, the most religious people on earth. Some 150 million people, well over half of the population of the United States, belong to churches. Has the government simply trampled on our rights as the religious majority stood by, victimized? Hardly. We have failed to take serious faith seriously. When surveyed, the majority of the American public rejects the notion of absolute truth, does not believe in the God described in the Bible, does not believe that Satan is a real being, believes all faiths teach basically the same thing, and does not believe it matters what god they pray to because every deity is ultimately the same deity, shrouded in different names and attributes of humankind.[1]

Clearly, this is not the radical and transforming faith required for such a time as this. Rather, it is a faith devoid of true meaning and devoid of hope of finding true meaning. We should not be surprised then to find ourselves with a village such as we have today—with a citizenry like we have today.

One of Christ's main warnings was of the uselessness of salt should it lose its saltiness. We are called to be the salt and the light of this world. If we do not do it, who will? As Francis Schaeffer has written in *Escape from Reason*,

> We have come to a fearsome place where the word *Jesus* has become the enemy of the person Jesus, and the enemy of what Jesus taught. In churches where abortion is just an option, adultery is accepted and truth is relative, God is a word. This contentless banner bearing the name *Jesus* must be opposed because we love him.

We need to learn the lesson of Paul on Mars Hill. A barren strip of land high above the city of Athens was the site of the powerful Areopagus. At its height of power, the Athenian Council met there to pronounce justice. By the time of Paul's second missionary journey, however, the council had lost much of its legal power. Nevertheless, it considered itself the custodian of teachings that introduced new religions and foreign gods.

Here, Paul was able to give one of his most famous sermons (Acts 17:22–31), because he had an understanding of historical and recent Athenian society and he understood the current thinking of the day. Likewise, for the church of today, and for those who wish to transform our culture, we must understand what is happening in our culture and in our society. This means that we must be *a part of society.*

Addressing the Southern Baptist Pastors' Conference, Tony Evans said,

> We are not in the mess we are in in America because sinners are sinning. Sinners are *supposed* to sin. If you are born in sin, shaped in iniquity, and are by nature the children of wrath, sin is what you do. Some can do it better than others. Our tragedy is not that sinners are sinning. Our problem is that the saints who are not supposed to be like the sinners who sin are often more sinful than the sinning sinners of sin.

What, then, should the church do? I am not a theologian, I am not a preacher, and this is not meant to be preachy, but I am convinced that we should first return to the basics. We have contained in the pages of Holy Scripture the answer to most of life's questions. In them we have a picture of the kind of Father that we serve. We are able to come face-to-face with the Living Christ. We see that the God of our help in ages past is also the God of help and hope yet to come. Those truths must be the mantra of our existence. They need to be preached from every pulpit, proclaimed by every believer, and lived by Christ's people.

Francis Schaeffer showed how small changes in thinking perverted the arts, philosophy, science, entertainment, and eventually theology. I am convinced that it is our task to show how a change in our understanding of the role of the church can result in an even greater change in all of those areas.

To do that, the Church needs to be clear. Many are teaching, either overtly or covertly, that God is still dead, truth is dead, that we cannot *know* truth, or that even if we could, it does not matter, because sincerity counts. That must change. We need to hold ourselves and our brothers and sisters in Christ accountable for what we preach.

If we believe that Christ is the answer, we need to be where the questions are being asked. There is a great quantity of writing recently on why some people believe we are raising a generation of people who do not know the difference between right and wrong. Perhaps it is because in those of us who call ourselves Christians, they see actions that make us no different from them. Perhaps they look at us and see that we have no more answers to our country's complex problems, no more love, no more compassion, and no more commitment. That must change.

As Schaeffer wrote nearly a generation ago in *Escape from Reason*, "The[re are] people ... in total desperation. We are fighting for our lives. If we love people, this is no age for a lack of comprehension, no age to play small-sized games, and no age to fall into the same thought-form of duality without realizing it."

A theology that does not flow into action is an irrelevant theology. Once we have come to grips with the importance of theology, truth, right, and absolutes, we will suddenly see had better hope that we do, for disaster waits not far down this road.

There is an old hymn that says, "We have come this far by faith,/Leaning on the Lord." It is, I think, indicative of the view of the importance of the church. Many people do not understand the historical context of the black church. The church in the African-American community plays quite a different role from the part it plays in the broadest culture. During slavery, it was illegal for groups of blacks to congregate, with one exception—church. So the church became the social, political, and economic center of the community. Therefore, if it did not happen in the black church, it just did not happen. That is why so many political leaders today in the black community are ministers. Almost every chapter president of the NAACP today is a minister. Many of our political leaders are ministers. Many of our college presidents were pastors.

It has always been an irony to me that the "religious right" has come under so much attack for being involved in politics when the black community has been doing it for hundreds of years. The Reverend Jesse Jackson is rarely, if ever, attacked for his involvement in politics. Dr. Pat Robertson is constantly attacked. Black church culture and black political culture are so interwoven. I do not think it is possible for a black politician to give a political speech without an Old Testament reference. In one sense, the black church has been a far more relevant factor in transforming culture than has the white church. Of course, the black church is allowed to influence culture, while the white conservative church is criticized for attempting to influence culture.

One of the places where I see Christ's commands trampled on is in the divide between the black church and the white church. Despite the lip service paid to their working together and sharing together, more often than not, that occurs maybe once or twice a year. Every so often, a black minister will show up in the pulpit of a prosperous suburban church, and every so often a white minister will show up in the pulpit of an inner-city church. When this happens, it is very likely that the visiting pastor will talk over the heads of the respective congregations. The black pastor will likely mention something about the evils of poverty and racism. The white pastor will likely mention something about the horrors of abortion and homosexuality. The congregations will nod their heads politely and say, "I cannot wait till our pastor is back next week."

There is a gulf between white and black churches. The black church has as a goal the elimination of racism and poverty. The white, mainstream, conservative evangelical churches have as their goal the elimination of homosexuality and abortion. As a result, they keep missing each other. As someone who is a "bridge" person, I am trying to convince the black church to stand for righteousness on the issues of abortion and homosexuality, while at the same time challenging the white church to be involved in and care about eliminating racism and poverty.

We have heard much talk in recent church history about the "full gospel." What that traditionally meant was whether the church was going to practice all the fruits of the Spirit. The reality is that the "full gospel" of things confronting today's churches is not just abortion and homosexuality for the white church and poverty and racism for the black one—it is the "full gospel" as played out in all of these issues. If the church cannot model for the world what the kingdom looks like, there is no hope. Because racism's seeds are so tiny, buried at a person's core, I believe the only means to clean out that seedbed is the magical and mystical working of the Holy Spirit in someone's life.

An active, committed church can transform America, but it will not be just through letter-writing campaigns to Congress.

(Please do not stop writing.) That may bring about political change, but to really transform America, we must *be* Christ's ambassadors to a hurting, dying culture. Our embassies should be open and offering love and practical help to the people of our village. When we minister to a dying AIDS patient, people will believe that we "hate the sin but love the sinner." When we take in foster children and raise them as our own, the world will know that we care about children *after* they are born. When we feed and shelter the homeless, then it becomes believable that we care for the least among us.

When congregations all over America start *living* the gospel in a sacrificial way, we can transform this culture without having to pass a bill or elect a president to do it for us.

1.   George Barna, *The Barna Report: Absolute Confusion* (Ventura, Calif.: Regal Books, 1993).

Chapter Eight

Education

"*Turn the station back on!*"

"*No.*"

"*Turn it back on now . . . or else!*"

"*Get lost.*"

"*I'm serious!*" He did not know what he was thinking. It was a camping knife, a Boy Scout knife. He opened it up in an instant and lunged. His thrust found its target with a sickening crunch. So hard was the stab that the blade of the little knife broke.

The nausea began in his stomach and progressed rapidly up and down his body. He began to shake. The other boy did not know what had happened. His friend had tried to stab him with a knife. The blade broke. . . . He looked down, expecting to see blood. There was none. . . . The belt buckle . . . Ben had stabbed the belt buckle. He turned around and ran. The radio flew to the ground behind him. Ben just stood there, the stub of the knife in one hand, the transistor radio's muffled cry on the ground in front of him. He turned around and ran.

His mama was almost as young as he was. She had been married at thirteen; she had a third-grade education and held down three jobs. She did not know what to do with young Ben, either. He and his *brother were doomed to make the same mistakes she had made, her husband had made, her brother had made, and so many other black young men and women had made.*

One day, she had had enough. Tired of seeing the blank expression on her sons' faces, she said that TV could only be watched two or three times a week and that often only if they had read and completed two book reports.

"Book reports?!" Ben thought that was the most idiotic thing he had ever heard. Didn't she know what the kids would call him? "Nerd." "Poindexter." Or maybe worse. But you did not mess with Sonya. The law of Sonya stood, or she stood on you, he would recall later.

Off he trudged to the Detroit Public Library. He did not know what he wanted to read. He hated school. He was the "class dummy." But sports ... maybe sports. Sports sounded interesting. She did not tell him what to read, only to read. So he decided that he was only going to read about the things that interested him. The first books and reports were done, and Mama was happy. The days and weeks went by, and soon he began to discover that there were many interesting things in those books. With no money to buy anything or go anywhere, the pages in between the covers of those books allowed him to go places. He could do anything. He could meet anybody. He could be anybody.

School began to be fun, and by the time he entered Wilson Junior High, he was at the top of his class. Kids who had once teased him and called him "dummy" now asked for his help on homework.

The worst experience, though, came at the time of his greatest triumph. He had been chosen the outstanding student for the eighth grade. His teacher publicly berated his white classmates for allowing him, a black, to win an award for outstanding student. But he never gave up.

Today, Dr. Ben Carson is the author of two books. A graduate of Yale University and the University of Michigan, he is a motivational speaker. The father of three children, he is one of the world's best neurosurgeons. At age thirty-three he was named Chief of Pediatric Neurology at Johns Hopkins University. In 1987, he was the lead surgeon on a team that separated Siamese twins joined at the head. Ben credits his mother and his education for his attainments.

One of the questions I am frequently asked is, "How did you do that?" "How did you go from being born on a kitchen table in the slums of Portsmouth, Virginia, to serving in federal and state government?" After a discussion of faith, a discussion on education quickly follows. It is a discussion that begins with the historic realization that faith and education have always been the cornerstones of the black experience. There are a number of Sonya Carsons out there—numerous women who work three or four jobs to make ends meet but do so with the hope that their labor will provide enough for their children to thrive. Most of these women, like Sonya Carson, are not educated, but that lack of education is more than compensated by a maternal desire to see their children excel.

When African-Americans were freed from slavery, one of the first tasks that people set about to do was create institutions to educate and train. There were people like Samuel Chapman Armstrong. A Union general who felt a commitment to educating the freed slaves, he helped found a school that today is known as Hampton University. Hampton, like many historically black colleges and universities, helped to prepare African-Americans for this complex and difficult thing called freedom.

One of the miracles of our survival was a high school known as Dunbar High School in Washington, D.C. From 1870 through 1955, Dunbar was an all-black public high school.

It was also an institution for the academic elite. Even in 1899, Dunbar students came in first in city-wide tests given both in black schools and white schools. During this eighty-five-year time frame, the majority of Dunbar's graduates went on to college though the majority of white and black Americans did not. While most graduates could only afford to attend federally sponsored institutions like Howard University, many also attended the most prestigious institutions this nation had to offer. Harvard, Yale, Amherst, and Oberlin all admitted Dunbar graduates. In fact, from 1892 to 1954, thirty-four Dunbar graduates attended Amherst. Seventy-four percent graduated, and more than twenty-five percent graduated Phi Beta Kappa.

The story did not begin with Hampton, and it did not end with Dunbar. In the years following the end of slavery, elementary schools, secondary schools, colleges, and universities sprung up in the South *and* in the North. Freedom from the captors required skills to be useful. Freedom of persons dictated an educated and free mind.

Our notion of what constitutes American education is, however, vastly different from the understanding of American education that our parents had. In turn, their views were different from their parents, and so on. American education is an evolutionary creature.

The American commitment to education was summed up well by the American educator Horace Mann, the father of the public school system, who said in 1848,

> And the greater the proportion of minds in any community, which are educated, and more thorough and complete the education which is given them, the more rapidly, through these sublime stages of progress, will that community advance in all the means of enjoyment

and elevation; and the more it will outstrip and outshine
its less-educated neighbors.

Education remained almost solely a state responsibility
until the National Elementary and Secondary Education Act of
1965, which involved the federal government first at the level
of school programs in poor urban areas. Since that time, the
intrusion of the federal government into the daily lives of school
children has increased greatly.

Since that time, perhaps coincidentally, the quality of
American education has decreased. The most sobering assessment of the absolute dearth of knowledge circulating among our
children came from a 1986 assessment of nearly eight thousand
seventeen-year-old high school students. On history questions,
the students answered, on average, 54.5 percent of the questions
correctly. On literature questions, only 51. 8 percent. (When I
went to school, any score below sixty-five was considered failing.) What this report makes clear is that we are now failing our
children.

Some of the specific results: More than thirty percent of
all students did not know that Columbus reached the New
World before 1750. Forty percent did not know that the Constitution was written between 1750 and 1900, and a similar
number did not know that the attack on Pearl Harbor occurred
between 1939 and 1943. Thirty-four percent of students, when
given a map of Europe, could not identify the country of France.
On other matters, nearly seventy percent of students could not
identify what the Magna Carta is. A third could not identify
that the Declaration of Independence is the document that
marked the formal separation of the colonies from Britain.

On the literary front, when asked what authors wrote
which works, only fifteen percent could identify de Tocqueville
with *Democracy in America*; only twenty-two percent could

match Henry James with *Daisy Miller* and *The Portrait of a Lady;* only thirty-six percent could place Geoffrey Chaucer with *The Canterbury Tales;* and only thirty-six percent identified Herman Melville as the author of such works as *Billy Budd,* "Benito Cereno," and "Bartleby the Scrivener." When asked about the characteristics and accomplishments of well-known authors and their works, only fifty-seven percent of students knew that Shakespeare wrote sonnets and plays. And fewer than two-thirds of all students knew that Aesop wrote fables. When asked questions about the literature of the Bible, nearly thirty-six percent of students identified Jesus' betrayer as either John, Pontius Pilate, or Mary, his mother. Forty percent of students said that Jonah was thrown into a lion's den, was shipwrecked for forty days and nights on an island, or that he killed a giant.

There were more than 250 questions in all, and with a few exceptions, they are roundly depressing. It should come as no surprise to anyone, though, that the same students watched television, did not read, rarely studied literature even in English class, and had little interest in education.

Not too long ago I had in my office a young African-American man who wanted a job. He had already interviewed with other people in the Cabinet, but he was yet to find a job. He thought that since he was black and conservative and I was black and conservative . . . well, you know, a match made in heaven.

I assigned a member of my staff to mentor him. His letter had typographical errors and was grammatically horrible. When I sat down and talked to him, he was offended. "Everyone else seems to think that my work is good." He went on to say that he had graduated with good grades from a fine university, that he had presented his thesis to a conference. Everyone told him that he was a good student with a good future. He wanted to know why I was being so hard on him.

I said, "I must be the only one who cares about you." I was the first person in his life who held up a standard for him. He was dumbfounded. He had tons of potential, but he was flawed. "I have the same standard for you that I have for anyone else in this office. Actually, you *are* getting preferential treatment; anyone else would have seen his letter filed in the trash can." We have done so much disservice to people like him.

Let us make something very clear: Our system is not in the shape it is in because we have not spent enough. The United States spends more each year per student on public elementary and secondary education than Canada, Italy, West Germany, France, the United Kingdom, and Japan. On public education alone, we spent more than $215 billion in 1992. For that money, a smaller share of the school dollar is now being spent on student classroom instruction than at any other time in recent history. Between 1960 and 1984, local school spending on administration and other noninstructional functions grew by 107 percent in real terms, almost twice the rate of per-pupil instructional expenses. During those same years, money spent on teacher salaries dropped from over fifty-six percent to under forty-one percent of total elementary and secondary school spending. The most money spent on education guarantees us only one thing: well-paid bureaucrats.

Think back to your own education. What is it that you can point to that really challenged and provoked you? What really stretched you to learn? Was it an expensive desk? A computer? Was it a textbook with glossy pictures? No, it was a teacher. It was an individual. It was a person. What we need more of is teachers who are excited about learning and who remember why they got into the profession in the first place. You can put that teacher into any classroom with the most menial of materials and he or she will produce scholars. You can also put a poor teacher in the best-equipped and best-funded classroom in history and provide every extracurricular activity and aid ever invented. And we have. And we have seen the results.

One of the single most important factors in changing our sick and dying culture, in rehabilitating the immune system of our nation, is to change the education system. It is easy to control masses of people who do not know how to read and write and think. It is far more difficult to control people who think, ask questions, and challenge. How different political campaigns would be if we would read policy papers instead of letting others feed us sound bytes.

This is not some cosmic revelation. Others have had it as well. An article in *The Humanist* clearly lays out the agenda of the radical left:

> I am convinced that the battle for humankind's future must be waged and won in the public school classrooms by teachers who correctly perceive their role as the proselytizers of a new faith: a religion of humanity that recognizes and respects the spark of what theologians call divinity in every human being. These teachers must embody the same selfless dedication as the most rabid fundamentalist preachers, for they will be ministers of another sort, utilizing a classroom instead of a pulpit to convey humanist values in whatever subject they teach, regardless of the educational level—preschool day care or large state universities.[1]

Amidst the squalor of American education today is the call for "outcome-based education" (OBE). Rather than grading kids on the cognitive outcome of what they know and what they do not know, some people believe that we should instead grade them on their efforts and their attitudes and their feelings. If we can do that, we are told, we can turn around the kids and the cities.

I was raised by a woman who did not need anyone to tell her that it is a terrible thing to waste a mind and that education is important. She even knew that self-esteem is important, but she advised me to get my self-esteem by learning the multiplication tables. She said, "If you can read and be excellent at what you do, they cannot stop you."

Fighting outcome-based education is important. We cannot raise children prepared to survive in our culture just by making them feel good about themselves and starting their days with group hugs. Children need to feel good about themselves because they can name all of the states, know their multiplication tables, spell, write essays, and speak persuasively—that will make them feel good about who they are and equip them to survive in our world.

One night Ben Carson was giving a speech. "Don't let anyone turn you into a slave. You are a slave if you let the media tell you that sports and entertainment are more important than developing your brain. You do not have to be a brain surgeon to be a valuable person," Dr. Carson said. "You become valuable because of the knowledge that you have. And that does not mean you won't fail sometimes. The important thing is to keep trying."

Today, Ben Carson is married to fellow Yale graduate, Candy Rustin. They live outside Baltimore with Sonya and their three sons (Murray, Ben, Jr., and Rhoeyce). Carson tries to spend as much time at home as possible. "I don't want my kids to grow up with no father like I did," he says. "I came to the conclusion a while ago that you can work until midnight and not be finished, or you can work until 6:00 or 7:00 and not be finished. I decided I'd rather work until 6:00 or 7:00."

Carson is raising his sons according to the laws of Sonya: two books a week, plus reports. He knows that her scheme works, he says. "A lot of the kids I grew up with are dead from drugs and violence." His mission in life, he believes, is to help others—particularly blacks. "It does not matter if you come from the inner city. People who fail in life are people who find lots of excuses," he says. "It's never too late for persons to recognize that they have potential in themselves."

Do you want to transform America? Then you must be involved in education reform. Make sure that your issue is heard and counted when education policy is being debated. That means PTA and school board meetings. But it also means much more than that. It means encouraging, supporting, and rewarding excellent teachers, and challenging those who view their profession as nothing more than a job. It means serving on the textbooks and curriculum committees. We do not have the option of abandoning our public schools. *We cannot transform America without a virtuous, educated populace.* Whether you choose to home-school your children or not, you still have a responsibility to be involved in public education. We cannot retreat into our homes. The children who are left behind are the future neighbors, politicians, bosses, friends, leaders, doctors, and spouses of our children. We *all* have a vested interest.

1.   John J. Dunphy, "A Religion for a New Age," *The Humanist* (January/February 1983), 26, found in Thomas Sowell, *Inside American Education: The Decline, the Deception, the Dogma* (New York: MacMillan, 1992), 59.

Part 2

We have spent the first half of this book looking at the state of the village. We have seen its weaknesses and the opportunistic infections ravaging its system. But we have also seen what the institutions of the village *should* look like, what strong individuals, families, schools, churches, and communities mean to a strong country.

We now turn from diagnosis to application. Here is where we put it to the test. I have chosen from the many issues facing our nation. These are not the only issues of importance, but they have been the subject of much analysis and debate. They are *abortion, homosexuality, racism,* and *poverty.*

Interestingly, these four issues divide not only the country, but they divide families and churches as well. Typically, those who are concerned about the abortion issue are interested in the moral implications of homosexuality and vice versa. And just as typically, those who advocate on behalf of the poor usually care a great deal about racism and vice versa.

These two camps are easily identifiable. They should not be. The former camp is made up mostly of whites, conservatives, and Republicans. The latter camp is mostly blacks, liberals, and Democrats. Oh, yes, and in case you were wondering, there are Christians in both camps. We are usually peeking across the barbed wire doubting the virtue and indeed the salvation of those camped at the other end of the ideological spectrum.

At the point of Calvary all these issues are important. They all matter. This then is the section where we talk about all four and try and convince each camp to pull down the barbed wire and to fight side by side, or at least not to fight each other. Others will know we are Christians by our love, except, of course, if we disagree politically or ideologically. Then they will know us by the venom we spew at each other.

The criticism usually goes only to the religious right. "Bigots," "intolerant," "hateful"—those labels get slapped on quickly and usually when we are winning debates and scoring points against liberals.

I must tell you, however, that as I travel back and forth between both camps I find those same labels get taped to the chest of those on the religious left—usually when we are demanding justice and equality for the poor and fighting against racism and sexism.

Oops! Did I say "we" both times? How could this be? And I thought Kay was one of us! For years Charles and I thought that we were cultural misfits, exhausted as we tried to stop abortion and end poverty. There was nothing novel about a black couple who wanted to end racism. But boy, did the invitations roll in to speak about abortion and gays in the military.

Charles and I have long ago decided that we are called to be bicultural bridge people. Traveling back and forth, translating, challenging, and encouraging both camps, we also recognize the danger that we're in. Bridge people sometimes get walked on by both sides. We do have a few footprints on our backs. After I spoke out on behalf of the unborn, a black pastor accused me of being a "surrogate of the right wing." After admonishing a suburban white church to become involved in helping the unborn poor there were those who complained about having to listen to that left-wing gibberish!

For the black urban Christian dealing with all the problems of poverty and racism, I hope this will help you to understand why the issues of abortion and homosexuality matter as you fight the battles God has called you to. And to the suburban white Christian who has dedicated years to stopping the slaughter of unborn children, I hope that you will come to understand the battlefronts that have preoccupied your black brothers and sisters.

If I had a dollar for every time I have been asked, "Why aren't more blacks involved in the pro-life movement?" I could finance my children's college education. I have long since stopped answering that question. I usually pose another: "Why are not more whites involved as *activists* to end poverty and racism?"

For everyone reading this section, hopefully there will be things that challenge you. For those who know and understand the great horrors of abortion and the destructive nature of the homosexual lifestyle, those chapters here will serve to reaffirm your commitment to be involved in these issues today. But you might also find yourself confronted for the first time with the realities of racism and poverty that exist in America. What we must all confront is that we are blind to certain problems and certain needs in America. *If* we are brave enough to admit that and brave enough to look for what is right, we will find the strength to change our culture.

My hope in this section is that you will finish it convinced that at the point of Calvary all these issues are important. Clearly we cannot all focus on everything. But just as clearly, we must be able to see everything.

Chapter Nine

Abortion

[C]ontrary to established opinion, the disagreement over abortion is not, at root, a legal one. Law is neither the fundamental problem nor the final solution. Thus, if abortion rights advocates think that their opposition will just get tired some day and go away, they are dreaming—as are anti-abortion advocates if they imagine that all will be well the moment Roe v. Wade is overturned. None of the various possible legal outcomes will settle the dispute or even ease the tensions between these two groups, because the abortion controversy is in its nature a cultural controversy. No matter what happens in courts and legislatures the abortion issue will not disappear until we somehow reach a greater consensus with respect to the standards of justice and goodness our communities will abide by. If there is to be an abortion law that is politically sustainable over the long haul, then, the fundamental task must be one of moral suasion.

—JAMES DAVISON HUNTER
UNIVERSITY OF VIRGINIA

On a number of occasions I have heard the following story. I do not know whether or not it is true. If it is, it should be a model for the kind of love, sacrifice, an commitment that we need to embody. If it is merely a story, it should be a story that we strive to make a reality.

A pastor of a small-town church felt convinced of the need to devote time and attention to the abortion debate. He believed that a culture that threw many of its young into garbage cans or down garbage disposals was a culture in need of confronting. He prayed and he listened. As he did, an idea began to take shape in his mind: His little town had only one abortion clinic, only one abortionist. He decided that he needed to extend the love of Christ to that doctor.

For the next few months, the pastor spent much of his sermon time talking about the nature of sin and the need of sinners—he prepared the ground. Slowly he got to the point where he felt that the congregation was ready to be told about his conviction. So one Sunday he strode to the pulpit, fixed his eyes upon his parishioners, and said, "For months I have had a burden on my heart to minister to the lost and suffering in this town." The congregation nodded in agreement. "Therefore, I have decided to ask the physician who runs the local abortion clinic to visit our church. I expect him to be greeted with love, dignity, and respect." Amidst the gasps and the looks of utter betrayal and amazement, there were also some tears. Though a couple of people got up that day and never came back to that little church, there were many more who shared the pastor's vision.

Over the course of the next few days, weeks, and months, the pastor and the congregation befriended the abortionist. The doctor started trusting people, and the congregation gave him Christ's love. Slowly he became a regular church attendee as well as a frequent dinner guest to many church members' homes. Other church members offered him help with housework and advice about some marital troubles he was enduring.

Eventually, the pastor and elders had the opportunity to share the gospel with him. Without hesitation he committed his life to the Lord. The next day, he went to work and performed four more abortions.

Everyone was stunned. People left the church. The pastor questioned God. But still there remained a core of people who were deter-

mined to demonstrate the sacrificial love of God, praying for the pastor, the church, and the doctor, and continuing to meet the mundane needs of the abortionist's life. Days and weeks passed as more and more preborn children's lives were terminated, all at the hands of a man who had asked God to be Lord of his life.

Then one day the veil was lifted. One day the doctor noticed a perfectly formed arm in the disposal tray. Suddenly this was not merely fetal tissue but a tiny human being. His grief was overwhelming. The pastor and the elders sat him down and prayed with him. They talked with him and let him know that his pain was just a portion of God's love for him. It was the searing cleansing love of a Savior.

Today, the doctor and his same staff run a small OB/GYN clinic in that small town. He is helping to bring babies into the world, not helping take them out of it.

It was 1969 and she was a poor young woman in Texas who wanted to have an abortion but could not, because they were illegal. They were a bunch of attorneys who had been looking for a test case to challenge the existing abortion laws. The two parties met. They made up a story—she would say that she had been raped by three men and a woman. It was perfect—a poor rape victim who wanted to rid herself of a horrible burden. Because her case was not resolved in time, she gave birth to the baby. Four years after that first meeting, she read in a Dallas newspaper about the Supreme Court decision bearing her pseudonym.

In 1989, a journalist located that almost-aborted "product of conception." She was now a beautiful young woman, inexorably opposed to abortion.

Abortion, despite the anger, the debate, and the passion, is not the issue—"abortion" is merely a medical procedure. As horrible as it is, abortion is just a symbol and a symptom of a greater problem. *The issue in this debate is how we view the value and the dignity of human life:* Is it a gift from God to be held in awe and reverence? Or is it a product of an intensely personal biological function with no real meaning? The answer to that question has implications not only for abortion but for how we view homosexuality, racism, and poverty, as well. For if we believe that life is more than happenstance, that life is a gift of a holy and sovereign God, then we *must* treat it as a holy and sacred gift, one to be revered, not compromised.

Abortion, however, provides an interesting context in which to trace this devolution of life. When I first started debating the life issue in the late '70s, the issue was whether or not that life inside the mother was actually life. Those who argued in favor of abortion would say, "It's not life. We are simply removing the product of conception." I always countered, "If it is not life, then you do not have to kill it. Just let it go on not living inside of you and we will all be fine. You will be spared a painful and invasive procedure. Taxpayers will be spared paying for a useless operation. The nonlife will go on being a nonlife—unless it actually starts growing and moving and living, in which case we have an entirely different problem and we will all be fine." I never lost a debate on these terms.

Science and technology eventually eclipsed the debate. In a lab somewhere, scientists gathered around a petri dish. They took an egg, took a sperm, and let them do their thing and . . . what do you know, it *was* a life! The terms of debate changed slightly. My opponents would say, "Yes, it's life, but it is not 'real human' life" —not an altogether insane argument but an imminently *flawed* one. I could say, "Okay, if it is not 'real human' life, you do not have to kill it. Leave it alone and see what it becomes.

After all, if it is not human, it may grow up to become a carrot, a turnip, an ear of corn, or perhaps a chair. On the other hand, it *may* grow up and surprise you. Because it is *real . . . human . . .* life. It has the *unique* genetic makeup of a human being that is unlike anything or anyone else in all of human history. You cannot just throw it away and get another one just like it. It is a special human being. It has everything it needs to love and live and breathe among us. So if it is not a human life, you do not know what it is. We are not going to add anything to it or take anything from it to make it human life. Everything it is going to be is determined right there from the moment of conception."

"Okay," they confessed, "it is human life."

The argument then became, "We know it has the genetic makeup of a human being, but it really does not become human and is not real life because it cannot feel pain, is not a contributing member of society, and does not have consciousness." That caused me *real problems.*

I would say, "Wait a minute, let me get this straight. I, Kay James, a *black* woman, am supposed to accept that one can define someone out of the human family just because one wants to? That does not work for me. Someone once tried to define *me* out of the human family, too. In *Dred Scott,* the U.S. Supreme Court decided that blacks were not members of the human family. The court found that blacks were not 'citizens.' So you might understand why this argument makes me very nervous. That some folks sitting in some black robes at the Supreme Court can decide who is a human being and who is not might not bother you, but it sure does bother me!—because I do not know whom they will decide to define out of the human family next. It could be you. They could decide that after you pass the age of sixty-five you are not human anymore because you are not contributing to society. You may think that this is impossible, but remember the former governor of Colorado who said that 'old people have a duty to die so that room can be made for the next generations'?" They rolled their eyes.

So they changed the debate again. "Until a child is viable, abortion should be safe and legal."

I would say, "What is 'viable'?"

"Until it can live independently of its mother," they would respond.

"Well, then, there go college kids. I do not know about you, but I did not bring my kids home from the hospital, sit them down in the baby carrier on the kitchen table, and say, 'There is the refrigerator, your room is down the hall on the left, the washing machine is downstairs, and oh, be careful, because on the warm cycle it tends to overfill.' My college-aged kids are *still* not completely independent."

Far from a victory, however, those favoring abortion then shifted the terms of debate to unprecedented ground. They said (and I will never forget the first time this happened), "We know that it is life, but we have tough choices that we have to make, and when it comes down to either the fetus's life or the mother's life, we think the life of the mother should be preeminent."

My response was only, "Why, because she is bigger? To me, this is a matter of civil rights. The babies are being discriminated against because of size, age, and place of residence. Does this sound familiar?"

They acknowledged that and said, "Yes, it's a tough choice, but it must be made." This was a moment of monumental importance, yet it was also a moment that slipped past most people's focus.

People started arguing for the ability of one person to take the life of another person. No longer was it a matter of "it is not life, therefore we can do with it what we please." Suddenly it became "it may be life, it does not matter, it's our choice." We were acknowledging that we are taking human life.

When the debate moved to this point, conceding that they were killing human beings, all God's people, black and white, should have gone to the mat. Most did not. Only the pro-life activists did. People now need to understand that we are at a point in our civilization where we know we are reaching inside mothers and killing their unborn children. We are admittedly killing another human being, and people are saying, "That's okay." Now, years after the American public acceptance of this notion of choice, we are losing the political debate. But the moral and ethical "high ground" still belongs to those who believe in the sanctity of life.

In the black church, I think we need to explore the gravity of this issue a little more closely. As we discussed earlier, abortion is not wrong because it is a medical procedure. It is wrong because of what it says we believe about human life.

The black church, more than any group should recognize this. Our current debate over choice is a stupid debate. I am not willing to concede that there ought to be a choice. I believe that in a free and civilized society there ought to be things about which there are no choices. Rape, murder, owning slaves, destroying preborn children, and a host of other crimes prevalent in our society ought not be choices. Let's review a little bit . . .

Since 1973, there have been nearly thirty million abortions in the United States. Every year, there are about fifty-five million abortions worldwide. How many is that? It means that around the world, 150,685 children are killed by abortion every day. Every hour, 6,278 children are killed. Every minute, 105 are exterminated. The numbers for the United States are smaller in magnitude but not in significance. Every year, 1.6 million unborn children are denied the right to life. Broken down by days, that means 4,383; per hour, that is 183; and it means 3 per minute. By 1973, 744,600 abortions were performed. *By the turn of the century, we will have killed thirty times more children through abortion than the number of Americans lost in all of our nation's wars—from the Revolutionary War to the Vietnam War.*

This has been done amidst ignorance. In a major study of abortion conducted by the Gallup organization, it was discovered that the American public fails to understand our nation's laws on abortion. Let's end that right now: *Roe v. Wade* and *Doe v. Bolton*, along with other court cases and legislation, permit abortions to be performed through the ninth month of pregnancy. That's it. That's the bottom line. There is no fuzzy area. If you want a ninth-month abortion, you can get it.

What is abortion? How is it done? Either by using a powerful vacuum to rip the child out piece by piece; or with a very sharp knife that dismembers the child; or with a saline injection that kills the child by burning it to death.

The results are not pretty for woman or for child. Physical and psychological trauma as a result of abortion has been well-documented. It is, no doubt about it, a horrible procedure. But as we said earlier, it is more than that as well.

Make no mistake about it, we did not arrive at this point in our history by accident. The "pro-choice" movement has been organized. And in the past thirty years, it has succeeded in changing the conscience of a nation. They sought first to identify the likely areas of strongest opposition. After concluding that it would likely come from the Roman Catholic church, they systematically tried to get the support of mainline Protestant denominations. They were highly successful. "Religious" groups developed, like the Religious Coalition for Abortion Rights (RCAR), with members such as the Presbyterian Church, USA, the Society of Friends, and others. RCAR soon became a player by pushing the slogan, "Prayerfully Pro-Choice."

The next move was to frame the issue in the terms of women's rights. They had much success there in tacking on the abortion platform to an existing platform of women's rights and women's freedom. As one Planned Parenthood representative said, "Our goal is to be ready as educators and parents to help young people obtain sex satisfaction before marriage. . . . By sanctioning sex before marriage, we will prevent fear and guilt."

How can we turn this movement around? Let's adopt the strategy of the opposition. First, we need to refocus the debate on life. Choice is about thirty-one flavors of ice cream and a dozen different TV and VCR selections; "choice" is *not* about who lives and who dies. Let's keep the focus there.

Second, we must recognize that while abortion may be the banner issue, the stakes are really far broader than that. The issue is really about restoring the nation's high regard for the value of human life. To do that, we need to change our culture and our attitudes. If we do, we will not only recapture all of the ground that we have lost, but we will also move forward to a time when human life is again respected as the beautiful creation that it is—life that should be greeted with love and admiration, not fear and trepidation.

Education is one of the keys to creating a world that values life. This requires us to go back. Back to holding small meetings in the basement of churches and homes, showing pro-life movies and videos. Back to convincing one person at a time, one part of the village at a time, that we are not talking about choice, we are talking about life and death. The two are wholly unrelated. One is eternal and human. The other is temporal and conceptual.

As we are involved in caring for women, adopting children,

praying for those involved in the abortion industry and *genuinely* loving them as Christ does, we can change how the culture views this issue. We can change the culture as we continue to change the politics of abortion.

We need to look inside ourselves as well. The fundamental question for an individual becomes, "How do I view the dignity and sanctity of human life?" The radical answer will dictate how we live. The radical answer also has something to say not only about how we feel about abortion, but also about how we treat the busboy who is serving us in the restaurant. It has something to say about how we view and how we treat people of different color. It has something to say about how we view and how we treat people who are homosexual. It has something to say about how we view and how we treat people who are the poor, weak, and disabled among us. We cannot have a high regard for the dignity and the value of all human life and be a racist, a homophobe, and immune to the plight of the poor.

This applies to the murderers of abortion doctors David Gund and John Britton as well. The second that those men pulled the trigger, they stripped themselves of the pro-life credibility. In abortion, pro-choicers argue that they have the right to choose who lives and who dies. It's a "woman's choice." Tragically, those who killed the abortionists thought that the choice was theirs to make, but one cannot be pro-life and pro-death at the same time—but a few are.

Want to know what else you can do? Did you know that for every abortion clinic that exists in America today there is a crisis-pregnancy center that is designed to help those same women and those same children? Volunteer at a crisis-center program and involve the entire family. Learn to staff a hotline. Donate money, food, and time. Consider sharing your home with teenage mothers and their babies. Consider being a foster parent, coaching girls in labor, helping with college tuition, providing transportation. Even consider adopting unwanted children.

Remember the story of the doctor near the beginning of this chapter? What makes this story unique is what makes this story possible. The change came about not as the heroic results of a single person. It came about because of the absolute determination of many different individuals and groups. It is the illustration of the village analogy.

The pastor was convinced. He prayed as an individual and as a church leader for God to reveal what He wanted him to do. His church responded as a body with love for the abortionist. The families in the church took him in, loved him, and cared for him. His business accepted his change and supported him in his new venture. And even in this story there are dozens of people who do not receive attention or credit but who were vital to changing this small culture and this small community.

This small change can be replicated in town and city across this country. There are many who already practice a pro-life culture. This encouragement is not meant to ignore your contributions but to encourage others to join you. Hopefully, we will suddenly find people looking at us in a different way. They may not agree with us, but they will know in their hearts that we are real. That we care. And this will matter. It will matter when we vote. It will matter when we protest. It will matter when we testify. It will matter when we debate. Because we will be carrying the mark of the servant and not the master.

If you doubt that this is important, imagine that the pro-life movement folds its tent and goes away. Imagine that there is no longer anyone out there who is defending the value and the sanctity of human life. Where will this country be in ten years? Not only will there be rampant abortions and children dying, but there will also be assisted suicide, euthanasia, and infanticide. Before you say, "She's lost her mind," know that there has actually been legislation introduced, at the state level, that proposes that there should be a three-day period before deciding whether a child should live or die. The legislation was introduced under the auspices of the "tough cases" of birth defects and severe disabilities, but the reality is the same.

Now imagine that we could declare a victory. Imagine that we could snap our fingers and declare overnight that everyone has respect for life. What would our nation look like? What would the implications be? If every human being were to have high regard for the dignity and value of human life, what would the implications be on acts of violence? What would the implications be for a drug dealer pushing death on his community if he has a high regard for the dignity and value of human life? What would the implications be for people in their sexuality if they really care for and hold in high esteem their partners? The implications would be profound—profound enough for us to sacrifice all that we are and all that we have to see that victory become a reality.

Chapter Ten

Homosexuality in America

Years ago, I debated a lesbian on the abortion issue. As usual, the debate was intense. She argued for choice. I argued for closure on what the contents of the womb are during pregnancy. She argued that as a professing Christian, she could not see making those kinds of choices for other people. I argued that as a professing Christian, I felt I had an obligation to care for all life, preborn and born, young and old. We also touched on the issue of homosexuality. She said that she knew she was born that way. I said that I knew what God had to say about the gay lifestyle. We debated nurture and nature, gays and lesbians, life and death. In front of hundreds of people, we both laid it on the line. When the debate was over, I went over, hugged her, got very close to her face, and said, "I hope I see you in heaven." Through the incredulous look on her face she said to me, "You think I can be in heaven?" I said, "If I can be, why not you?"

Years later she wrote a letter to a friend of mine and told her how much that one exchange had meant to her. She had no doubt about how I felt about her lifestyle, but she also had no doubt how much I loved her. Absent that love, however, I have no credibility to talk to her.

Taken corporately, conservatives and Christians have little credibility on homosexuality. Of the many things that are prevalent in the debate over homosexuality, love has not been one of them. Certainly there is much about the homosexual *agenda* that we *should* fear.

We have been hearing for years that ten percent or more of the entire population is gay. The totality of that evidence is based on a series of surveys done by sex researcher Alfred C. Kinsey. Collectively published as *Sexual Behavior in the Human Male (1948)* and *Sexual Behavior in the Human Female (1953)*, they have been used to justify special rights for homosexuals, the acceptance of homosexuals as normal and natural, and with that, a concession to their demands and their agenda.

For years, evidence from other countries, including Canada, France, Britain, Norway, Denmark, and other nations have consistently shown that about six percent of the entire population has had a homosexual *experience,* while less than one percent of the population is *exclusively homosexual.*[1]

New looks at that original Kinsey data show it to be uselessly flawed. A review of his research methodology showed that about twenty-five percent of Kinsey's fifty-three hundred male subjects were former or present prisoners, and a high percentage were sex offenders.[2] The subjects were not even close to being representative of the general U.S. population. Many respondents to the surveys were recruited from sex lectures, where they had gone to get the answers to their sex problems.[3] Other respondents had been recruited from the known homosexual population, and perhaps as much as four percent, or two hundred, of his respondents were male prostitutes.[4]

After the Ball: How America Will Overcome Its Fear and

Hatred of Gays in the '90s defines exactly how to achieve the homosexual agenda. Their strategies will sound familiar. "The main thing is to talk about gayness until the issue becomes thoroughly tiresome."[5] They are succeeding. Psychologist Ronald Federici says in a *Washington Post* article entitled, "Teens Ponder: Gay, Bi, or Straight?" that "everything is front page, gay, and homosexual.... Kids are jumping on it."[6] Think back to the gay march on Washington in 1993. Coverage was everywhere. Visualize the cover of *Newsweek* in 1993 about how "cool" the lesbians are today.

"You can forget about trying right up-front to persuade folks that homosexuality is a *good* thing. But if you can get them to think it is just *another* thing—meriting no more than a shrug of the shoulders—then your battle for legal and social rights is virtually won."[7] In that *Washington Post* article, teens testified to the victory of the gay machine: "Someone asked me what my sexual orientation was, and I found myself unable to tell them. I had just been going along assuming I'm heterosexual. Then I sat down to think about it and realized I could go either way" ... "You choose to love whomever you choose to love."[8]

Think about your own home, your own office, or even your own church. How many times has the issue of homosexuality come up only to have someone shrug his shoulders and say, "Each to his own," or "As long as I do not see it," or "What they do in their own time is their business"? If it were that simple, a shrug might be acceptable, but as we will soon see, it is *not* that simple and it is certainly not harmless.

"*Where* we talk is crucial.... It suffices here to recall that the visual media—television, films, magazines—are the most powerful image makers in Western civilization. For example, in the average American household, the TV screen radiates its embracing bluish glow for more than fifty hours every week, bringing films, sitcoms, talk shows, and news reports right into the living room. These hours are a gateway to the private world of straights through which a Trojan horse might be passed."[9] They also write, "The [gay] movement should eagerly ally itself with large, mainstream groups that can actually advance our interests (e.g., the Democratic Party, the National Organization of Women, or the Presbyterian Church). But even then, we should demand to see some major public demonstration of their commitment to our cause before we rush to commit to theirs."[10] On all counts they have succeeded. Think about the lesbian characters on *Roseanne* and *LA Law*—about the transvestite main character in *The Crying Game*—about Tom Hanks' Academy Award for his marvelous portrayal of a gay man dying of AIDS. Or think about the New York City mayoralty race. Lost in the Republican afterglow of the Rudolph Giuliani victory was the fact that on almost every social issue, Giuliani differed from incumbent Mayor David Dinkens *not at all*. In this year's New York City Gay-Pride parade, Mayor Giuliani marched front and center.

You may think that I am sounding overly alarmist, but consider for just a moment the movie *The Crying Game:* one long piece of very well-created propaganda in which a heterosexual man falls for a transvestite. There is a story told in the movie about a scorpion and a frog. The scorpion asks the frog for a ride across the lake on his back. The frog says, "No. If I do, you will sting me and I will die." The scorpion says, "But it is not in my best interest to do that, because if I sting you in the middle of the lake, we will both die." The frog ponders that thought for a moment and says, "Well, okay, I will give you a ride." So the scorpion gets on the back of the frog, and off they go. Halfway across the lake, the scorpion stings the frog. As they are both sinking to their deaths at the bottom of the lake, the frog turns to the scorpion and says, "Why did you sting me? We are both going to drown!" The scorpion responded with, "I couldn't help it. It's my nature." That story was the crux of the movie. Until someone pointed it out to me, I had missed the inference as well. But the whole movie was aimed at getting the audience to accept that homosexuality is nature, that it just cannot be helped, even to the point of death.

An integral part of the strategy is to make the platform appear moderate. "We only want what everyone else has," or "We do not want to be discriminated against." These are the pleas that have fallen on our sympathetic ears. But the platform of the *1993 March on Washington for Lesbian, Gay and Bi Equal Rights and Liberation* is anything but moderate. Although couched in the language of accommodation and equal rights, it contains the seeds of a social revolution. It "demands":

- safe, affordable abortion and contraception to be available to all people on demand, without restrictions, regardless of age
- legislation to prevent discrimination against homosexuals, transsexuals, transvestites, and cross-dressers in the areas of custody, adoption, and foster care and to define the word *family* to include the "full diversity of all family structures"
- legalization of same-sex marriages
- passage and implementation of graduated age-of-consent laws (such legislation would lift age restrictions on peer sexual activity)
- full and equal inclusion of homosexuals, bisexuals, and transsexuals in the education system, and inclusion of homosexual, bisexual, and transsexual studies in multicultural curricula

I go through this litany of strategy and platform not to

foster hatred but to identify the goals and strategy of a well-defined movement.

There is another recognition, though. While calling for compassion and care, too many Christians and conservatives have been practicing exclusion and ridicule. Because of our visceral reaction against homosexuals and the reality that we have not extended love and grace to the individual homosexual, we have no credibility to take on the political agenda. We have neither confronted the sin nor loved the sinner. On this issue, we have done nothing right. We have done more to mess up on this one issue than on every other divisive issue confronting us today.

We need to go back and scrutinize ourselves again. What is going on in our hearts? Why do we have such a problem with homosexuals? I have seen it more among men than among women. Men are far more insecure with their sexuality than are women. I say this as one of the most insecure people I know.

Someone once gave me a very important bit of advice about relating to people and audiences. People, in general, they said, tend to like people that they think like them. If you think that I hate your guts, there is no way that you are going to like me, or even let me near you.

People need to believe that we like them—whether it is dealing with someone we disagree with on the abortion issue, whether we are afraid of them because of their race, or whether it is someone we think is a sinful abomination—we *must* like them. There is a catch, however. Liking someone cannot be faked or the insincerity will be perceived immediately. We must genuinely care about people. We must genuinely like people. If we do, they will, no matter who they are, feel the warmth of friendship and care radiating toward them.

We must learn to separate issues, ideologies, policies, and personalities, and we must learn to separate the sin from the sinner. Perhaps nowhere is this more needed than in the current tribulations over the homosexual issue.

How can we minister to people we hate? If anyone understands this concept, a family member should. In most families there are disagreements galore, but also in each family there is much more than a veneer of love and grace. No matter how crazy Uncle Buck is, we still love him. We still want to spend time with him. We still want to know how he is doing. And when Uncle Buck stumbles, we still want to be there to pick up his crazy butt. We need to extend that same kind of care to *all* our brothers and sisters.

C. S. Lewis suggests that anytime you are in a crowd, look at the people on your left and look at the people on your right. And remember that in ten thousand years, one of those people might be a person so magnificent and glorious that you might be sorely tempted to worship him on sight. And remember that in ten thousand years, one of those people might be a creature so hideous that you could scarcely look at it.

We need to remember that every person and every homosexual we meet is the child of Almighty God—loved by Him as much as any other person in the history of humanity. How can we not love them? How can we not be willing to sacrifice for them all that we are and all that we have?

How can we as individuals, families, churches, and communities turn the tide of our debacle in dealing with homosexuals? We need to be where they are. Today, that often means that we need to be caring for the weakest among them: the AIDS patients. Some of these patients will be gay, others drug users, others innocent victims of a tainted blood supply, but they will all be people in need of care. And we will be watched. They will see in our hugs or our turned shoulders whether we love them. They will relay our actions and our hearts to their friends and families. And if the stories that they relay convey the love that is the Great Physician's, we will be viewed as people who care.

When we then confront them, in love, with the conflict between their life and the life God commands us to lead, they will not be able to counter with accusations about backwater faith with no relevance to our world. But we must also be ready to explain the sins in our life to them. To explain that an alcohol problem, or that bout of adultery, or that car that you covet, is not without the need for forgiveness as well—that our sins and their sins are equal, and that they all need forgiving.

For the churches, this means that all homosexuals should be welcomed, even encouraged to come. They should be greeted with the same respect and dignity afforded to every person created and shaped in the image of God. They should be supported in their times of need, and they should be ministered to. When it comes to joining the church, I think that questions should be asked—but not questions that separate them from any other sinner in need of the forgiveness of God. We must ask ourselves when someone walks down the aisle of the church or when someone says that he has asked Jesus to be his Lord and Savior, do we say, "Hallelujah, now please fill out this four-page survey about the sins in your life, so we may see if you are truly saved"? No, we do not. Nor should we with homosexuals. If a man or woman comes to the church and proclaims Christ as Lord, we should worship with, pray with, and hold him or her as accountable to the commands of Christ as anyone else.

That *may* mean confronting their gay lifestyle. It does not mean that the fact that they may have homosexual inclinations makes them special cases. Will they fall from time to time? I know I do in my sins, and I have never been kicked out of a church. If they reject the teachings of the faith, that is another story. But I believe we must not play judge and jury.

Our attempts at ministry to homosexuals should not be geared exclusively at converting them, inasmuch as our Lord taught us that we must often first meet physical and emotional needs before we can get to the spiritual needs. We must build bridges of concrete, not of words.

I think that the evangelical church in America has no credibility in the gay community. I know that when you preach righteousness, people are sometimes uncomfortable and antsy. And I sometimes hear that as a rationale for small congregations. But my experience is that churches that preach the truth, *in love,* need not sacrifice relationships and attracting people in numbers to proclaim the gospel.

A friend who happened to be a leader in a nearby church was dying of AIDS. When I last saw him, he was covered with open lesions. As we finished talking, I moved toward him to give him a hug. As I did, he pulled back. Without thinking, I said to him, "Don't do that to me." It was an odd thing to say to someone about to die, but I felt rejected when he pulled away. We eventually embraced, and it was the last time I saw him.

It taught me an important lesson. And so it should for us all. As Christians and as conservatives, we have been eloquent in our opposition to special rights for homosexuals, but in our eloquence, we have denied them that which we said they have: the *same* rights as everyone else. For families, this means that if there is a homosexual co-worker, he should be invited for cookouts and get-togethers just like everyone else. For homosexual neighbors it means that they get asked for a cup of sugar or an egg just like everyone else. We're not talking about preferential treatment, we're talking about the same treatment being given to any person who needs clothes, housing, help. We need to recognize that, regardless of their sinful state. We need, too, to recognize that there, but for the grace of God, go we.

To this church and in this day, the homosexual is viewed as the modern-day leper. The reason that one is gay is a very complex and difficult thing to understand, much as is someone who becomes an alcoholic, an adulterer, a drug addict or anything else sinful. But suppose we treated all adulterers, all those who engaged in premarital sex, all those who have had lustful thoughts of the opposite sex, all those who have been to a strip bar, with the same disdain and contempt with which we treat homosexuals?

Given the power of their political agenda, the force of their movement, and our failure to convey (or develop) our sincere love for all homosexuals, we must resolve ourselves to another long-term engagement. It is going to require a tremendous commitment as individuals, families, and communities.

As with every other area we are discussing, we must first search our own hearts. First, we need to get it "right." Though it is simplistic, the command to "do unto others" still applies. And until we do that, none of us should worry about commending it. Second, we should look for opportunities of ministry—there are many. Third, we should check our rhetoric. Those people who have unashamedly confronted the homosexuals on their agenda and on their lifestyle have not always done so in love.

When conservatives, political and religious, argue with such compelling language for the sanctity of human life, it really points out a flaw in our character if that language applies only to preborn children—if that applies only to women with a crisis pregnancy—if that applies only to cute white babies. If that language misses our gay brother or lesbian sister, *it calls the rhetoric and the messenger into question.*

1. For a more complete picture of these studies and the flaws of the Kinsey research, please consult "Homosexuals and the 10% Fallacy" written by J. Gordon Muir and appearing in the *Wall Street Journal* on March 31, 1993, A-14; *Kinsey, Sex, and Fraud* (Huntington House Publishers, 1990), "Only 1% of men say they are gay," *USA Today,* April 15, 1993; Robert Knight, "Sexual Disorientation: Faulty Research in the Homosexuality Debate," Family Research Council, June 1992.

2. J. Gordon Muir, "Homosexuals and the 10% Fallacy," *Wall Street Journal,* March 31, 1993, A-14.

3. Ibid.

4. Ibid.

5. Marshall Kirk and Hunter Madsen, *After the Ball: How America Will Overcome Its Fear and Hatred of Gays in the "90s,* (Doubleday, New York, NY: 1989), 178.

6. "Teens Ponder: Gay, Bi or Straight?" *Washington Post,* July 15, 1993.

7. Kirk and Madsen, *After the Ball,* 177.

8. "Teens Ponder," *Washington Post,* July 15, 1993.

9. Kirk and Madsen, *After the Ball,* 179.

10. Ibid., 182.

Chapter Eleven

Racism

After moving back to Richmond in the early 1980s, we tried Stoneypoint, a sister church to Grace Church in Roanoke, Virginia, hoping to find at least a handful of black families in the congregation. There were none, but we could not walk away from the teaching, fellowship, and evangelism that we found there. We decided to integrate the Presbyterians again.

A wonderful church, nevertheless, it, too, had its number of racial slights. When, eventually, we moved up to the northern Virginia area, it was very difficult to leave Stoneypoint Church—the church that had been such a nurturing environment when we had gone through the crisis of our daughter's nearly dying. Having all of our spiritual, emotional, physical, and financial needs met in Stoneypoint meant that we had a high standard for our next church. Like Grace Church, Stoneypoint was integrated basically because we went there. There had been some international families that came in and out, but it was far from a predominantly black church.

It was my desire, therefore, as we moved to northern Virginia, to find a church that was more black than any of our previous ones. This was important for Charles and me but even more important for our children. It was a very traumatic time for them. They had been *uprooted from family, from friends, from schools, from their communities. It was, therefore, very important for us to find a church in which they would feel comfortable. They were at a critical age where they were asking questions and when church youth groups and the church family was going to be more important in their lives. Up to that point, they had spent most of their church time being cared for in the nurseries; now they were all going to be in Sunday school, learning, worshiping, and, hopefully, making friendships that would last for life. While we visited a number of churches, both black, white, and gray, we did not find a place wherein we felt God was calling us to worship and fellowship. One Sunday, at the recommendation of some friends, we tried a church called McLean Presbyterian Church. Everyone told us what a wonderful place it was. It was . . . a wonderful disappointment.*

One Sunday in the late 1980s, we all ventured off to church together. Sitting through the service, I felt that the music was not all that it could be, but the congregation was another story. Before and after the service there were many people who searched us out and went out of their way to make us feel welcome. While the James family again stood out in the congregation, we were moved by the apparent warmth of the McLean Presbyterian family.

Things progressed nicely as Charles and I went off to our Sunday school class and Chuck, Bizzie, and Robbie each went off to theirs. At the end of a wonderful hour, we went off in search of our kids. Robbie was right where we left him. Bizzie, too. But when we came to the classroom where we had left Chuck, he was nowhere to be found. After much questioning and searching, we found him sitting outside under a tree near the church parking lot, not far from where our car was.

Chuck is probably the most affable, well-adjusted, easygoing, "I'm just happy to be alive," kid I have ever known. It takes a lot to set him off, because he is not easily offended. That Sunday, sitting under the tree, it was very clear that he had been offended. After much questioning and cajoling, the story began to stumble out of his mouth.

He had been happily playing with the other kids, learning about one of Jesus' miracles, when another child said to him, "Since when do they let niggers into this church?" In preparing the kids to come to this church, we had told them that this was going to be a great place, that the people who went here really loved God and would really love us, too. The build-up had been heavy with expectation and promise. The reality now bore the weight of a racial slight and lost innocence.

So there the James family sat, all five of us, under a tree, people streaming past, cars whizzing off to brunch, trying to explain how, in a church where we had told them that people loved God, such a comment could ever have been made. We had to explain to him the fact that such an incident was not unusual. That he would be confronting the same all of his life. The fact that it is sin. The fact that that child needed God's forgiveness just as much as Chuck needed God's forgiveness anytime that he did something offensive to God. We had to explain to him the realities of racism in modern America—the reality that the James family would experience blatant racism even in the late 1980s.

To date, we do not know whether that child who asked the hurtful question was visiting, or the child of a church elder. We did not go back to that church for months. In fact, every week we went to a new church in search of a home. Eventually, however, we went back, were again greeted warmly, again enjoyed the people, and ended up staying. We talked to the church's pastor that day, too, relayed to him the story, and watched as he recoiled in horror. For us, the story had a happy ending.

But what if we had not gone back?—had not confronted the church with the problem that we saw? Every day and every Sunday in America, people are shunned or offended or hurt by racism. How many of them simply walk away, turning their backs on white, black, *yellow, or brown America? How much pain is walking around today in our cities, our suburbs, our offices, our schools, our churches? A lot of pain.*

People always find it surprising to hear that Charles and Kay James are the victims of racism today. The really frightening thing, however, is not that Charles and Kay James have experienced racism—because we can put it in context. We cannot and do not blame racism for keeping us down. We cannot. We have "succeeded" in building for us and for our family the American dream. The frightening thing is that there are millions of poor blacks and poor whites who do blame each other. And that blame is deep. So is the pain.

Most racism in the church at least is not overt. Only rarely do I hear someone decry Martin Luther King, Jr.'s birthday as a holiday. Rarely do I hear someone mockingly break into black slang to show how stupid blacks really are. Much more common is the racism that accidentally shows a person's heart.

People will often say to me, "Kay, you are so wonderful, I do not see you as being black." I say, "You jolly well better. You see me as a woman. You see me as a pro-lifer. You very well better see me as black. Being black means something. Being black in America carries with it certain things. There is a heritage, a tradition, experiences, that come with being black. If you want to know me, want to understand me, want to be my friend, then you must want to know what being black is. No matter how uncomfortable it makes you. When you understand that, you understand me better."

Think about it, if someone came up to me and said, "Gee, Kay, you're great. I do not see you as being a woman," I would be offended. Especially if it meant that one day I am sitting in your living room and you walk by me in boxer shorts. That would offend me. I *am* a woman. Because of that, if I am a guest in your home, you should not walk through the house in your underwear, scratching your anatomy. The same is true of racism. It tells you something.

Before we bought our new house in northern Virginia, we got to know the people from whom we were buying the home. They knew that we were a tight family, and they wanted our kids to enjoy the home just as much as their own kids had enjoyed it when they were growing up. As we put the contract on the house and they prepared to move out, they had us over to dinner, had the kids over to swim in the pool, and made us feel more loved and welcomed than we had ever expected to feel when buying a house.

Shortly after we moved in, our black neighbors across the street came over to welcome us. Making some assumptions, they said to us, "Boy, are we glad you are here. This is such a conservative Republican neighborhood, and the people who lived here before you did were such racists." Charles and I looked at each other and said, "Well, we are conservative Republicans, Clarence and Ginny Thomas are two of our best friends, and we loved the people who sold us this house." As we revived them, we talked some more about the couple who lived in the house before we did. It turns out that several years ago, they had in their front yard one of those little black jockeys with a lamp. It flashed in neon lights across the front of their house for a black person passing by: RACIST. The reality is that they were anything but fire-breathing racists. But to the neighbors, the perception was reality. Because of that, they never spoke to each other.

We all need to be more aware of each other. All across America today there are battles about whether anyone should be allowed to display the "stars and bars," the rebel flag. Well, in my opinion, if it causes my brother to stumble . . . guess what? It should go. I have had the privilege of knowing people up close and personally who like their rebel flags, who fly their rebel flags, who have had rebel flags tattooed on their arm. But a white person with a rebel flag needs to understand that for ninety-eight percent of black people, that flag is going to say, "I am a racist."

That white person can argue all the day long that that is not what the flag symbolizes. I will even accept that. I accept that for many people who fly the flag, it carries absolutely no racial comment. I understand that it symbolizes states' rights and pride in the southern states and that it is a memorial to all the sons and daughters of the South who died fighting for those ideals. I know all of that. But what they need to know is that for black folks, it is a symbol of racism.

If the flag is flown because you do not understand what it symbolizes or because you do know what it symbolizes and you do not give a flip, we have a real problem. Symbols matter. Signals matter. Understanding the barriers matters. And once we understand those symbols, there is a choice to make. For me, that means that those symbols should go.

When we live in this place called America, this place where cultures bleed together, symbols matter. One of my roles in life is that of a bridge builder. To blacks I say, "These symbols do not necessarily equate with racism." To whites I say, "Please give it up."

We are talking about coming together. About living side by side. About rebuilding the village. It takes commitment and determination and sacrifice. Most people cling to their right to fly any flag that they want, or put any kind of statue on their lawn that they want, or wear a Malcolm X T-shirt, or fly the flag of the ANC (African National Congress). The fact is, we are called to give up everything.

When confronted with the topic of racism, most people in America today will acknowledge that, "Oh, yes we *did* have a problem with racism in our country. But that was years ago, and it occurred principally in the South." What is difficult, however, is for them to understand the problem of racism as it exists *today*. Most people that I run into in mainstream white America refuse to acknowledge that there is something known as racism that is alive and well in America today.

This racism crosses all economic boundaries. There is no amount of money that can make someone who dislikes you because of the color of your skin feel affection for you. For blacks that means that no matter how much you make, there are certain country clubs you cannot join and certain neighborhoods in which you cannot live. There are still certain churches where you will not be accepted. This is a pain of exclusion that is known only to those it affects.

Some of it, however, is displayed in the hatred and anger evident in rap music. Lyrics that extol murder, rape, torture, violence, and that tell stories of hopelessness, despair, and anguish are called by artists and critics alike the "pulse of a culture." That is a frightening thought. In a world where songs with lines like, "She begged me not to kill her,/I gave her a rose/Then slit her throat and watched her shake/till her eyes closed, /had sex with the corpse before I left her . . ." and titles like "I'm Your Pusher," and "F _____ the Police" are among the most popular, it should come as no surprise that hatred is rampant and that hatred is deep.

In 1992, when *Never Forget* was published, my publisher issued another book entitled *The Coming Race Wars: A Cry for Reconciliation* by Bill Pannell. So controversial was the book that many Christian bookstores declined to sell it. With a graphic depiction of racism as it currently exists, Bill said that unless we do something, we are headed for racial conflicts that will make the L.A. riots look like a boxing match in the park.

He is right. If we sit back and do nothing, there will be race wars in this country. (What did she say?) Race wars. Poverty and race do not have a one-to-one correlation. There are poor whites, poor blacks, poor Asians, rich Hispanics, rich African-Americans, and rich whites. Nevertheless, the proportion of poor blacks is significantly higher than the proportion of poor whites. If we do nothing on the race issue, then we will see that gap widen. The seeds of racial discontent in this country are obvious to anyone willing to examine them. The race riots of the 1990s differ from the race riots of the 1960s only in intensity. The lawlessness and hopelessness are the same.

Many of my Republican brothers and sisters have been eloquent in their denunciation of the L.A. riots. "Unrestrained lawlessness by hoodlums," "a bunch of thugs," and so on. The problem, they said, was not society; it was the action of a few individuals. They are mostly right. There is a deplorable amount of lawlessness going on in the inner cities. More and more people care less and less about everyone else, but there is more to the problem than simply the unrestrained efforts of a bunch of thugs.

We must ask ourselves why the riots were in the inner cities and not the suburbs. The answer clearly is that the inner cities are where the African-American males are. More specifically, the inner cities are where the *unemployed* African-American males are. The statistics are staggering. Today, thirty-six million people live in poverty in this land. About forty-seven percent of these people live in the central parts of our cities, compared with about thirty percent during the 1968 riots. Sixty percent of the country's black people who live in poverty dwell at the core of our major cities. Unemployment among inner-city blacks runs more than thirty-three percent. The feelings of utter hopelessness are even greater than that. Minds are numbed by the incessant blare of music that graphically mocks the value of human life, or television that tells them that they have the "right" to have certain things and have them *now*. We cannot ignore the societal dimension of these realities. I do not accept them as an excuse; neither can we ignore them as factors. Just as the immune systems of our general society are being decimated, so the immune systems of our inner cities are decimated. They are the brave new world.

The L.A. riots were not the last word: They are one of the foreshocks warning us of what is to come unless we get involved.

All parallels to the rise of the Third Reich should be viewed with a measure of skepticism. Nevertheless, one is appropriate here. The seeds of racial discontent in Germany had germinated for years. Every so often there would be ugly and isolated events that caused people to shake their heads and wonder what was going on. Few thought it a major problem, however.

Enter the economic factors. The constraints placed on Germany as a result of her aggression in World War I began to take a toll. Inflation started to rise. Germany's nationalist feelings were squelched as her military power was castrated. Unemployment rose. Soon, money that had been carefully saved for years could not even buy a loaf of bread. And just as surely as the masses began to suffer, someone was blamed. Those someones were the Jews.

"The Jews are ruining our country." ... "The Jews are taking our jobs." ... "The Jews have run this country and they are killing us." The venom rose as quickly as the rates of inflation. Into this furnace stepped a leader with the promise of a better tomorrow. A better tomorrow if—*if* the people gave up their rights—*if* the Jews could be stopped—*if* the Fatherland could reclaim what was rightfully theirs. Self-interest carried the day as it usually does in politics. On the "dirty Jews" and the "dirty foreigners" and the "unfit" and "unclean" were imposed the "final solution" to all of Germany's problems.

Clearly, I am not saying that we are headed for a holocaust in this nation. Just as clearly, I am saying that the seeds are always there in culture. The root of bitterness and the seeds of resentment are with us, and if there were changing economic conditions in this country, you could see "things" turn pretty nasty, pretty fast. When the gap widens between rich and poor, racial polarization is but a small next step. Bill Pannell was right when he wrote,

> I fear we may be headed into an America with little time to read. We are on the brink of a police state wherein law and order will mean something far more aggressive than it did when Richard Nixon inhabited the White House. If there is another urban uprising, it will not be a riot, but a war—one that could trigger W. E. B. DuBois's dark prophecy that the century would end in a devastating race war. Such a conflict has been simmering ever since the first boatload of slaves debarked on these shores. I hope we have come too far for something this disastrous to take place. But just in case, if we are going to get together, we had best do it quickly.

Quickly, quickly, quickly.

It is going to take a certain amount of effort and determination to do that. It is also going to take getting over the fear of being rejected. Because you will. Trust me, I know of what I speak. I was once one of those skeptical black women, but I was won over. If you want to do something about racism in America, recognize that even the smallest step, even the most basic friendship with a person of a different color may take years. The other stuff, the general, societal change that we seek, will take even longer. This is a battle for the generations and the ages, not the days and the weeks. It is not going to happen just during Black History Month when you take a black person to lunch and declare victory in race relations. It is not going to happen just by inviting a white person to your church and being able to say to yourself, "Boy, am I or am I not open-minded and liberal?" Going to lunch, inviting to church, sending a letter—these are important actions. But to change the destructive cycles that we are in—building relationships, taking chances, sharing vacations and lives—these are the undertakings with weight.

There are actions that churches can and should do, as well. Activities that are as big as the ministries that they choose to support and as small as the kind of Bible study materials that they use. Our church in Richmond, Stoneypoint, had a commitment to the core of Richmond and wanted to have a church that would be relevant to it and the people who lived there. They were so theologically pure and determined to remain that way that they did not make the effort to expand and learn about the culture they were living in, so that, to date, the church sits in the heart of black Richmond but has little if any impact on the community it is in. It is still the same white group of families with a good heart and good intentions but poor planning.

In the past thirty years, there has not only been "white flight" from the urban areas, there has been a "white stampede." But there has also been an abundance of "black flight" from the inner cities as well. The black middle class vigorously expanded and streamed into suburbs and formerly all-white urban neighborhoods. Left behind in the old, central-city ghettos was a residue of the unskilled—*the truly disadvantaged*—who faced the stark reality of a transformed, "deindustrialized" urban economy offering no employment for which they were qualified. Gone was the stable moral authority of many of the citizens who left. In its place was a desperate economic reality involving welfare dependency, crime, and underclass disorder.

One of the concerns that I have been thinking a great deal about lately is the need for families black and white to consider moving back to the inner cities of America. Today in the inner cities we have the closest thing to anarchy that exists in America. Black children grow up in the lawlessness, hopelessness, and violence that have come to define the inner cities. They are much more familiar with those realities than they are with the loving discipline of a father's love or the warm comfort of a gentle bedtime story. All too often the children of our inner cities grow up without ever experiencing beauty in their lives.

Unless we are there, how can we expect to change things? Unless we are there proving to the needy in the inner cities by our very presence that we love them, how can we expect to change things? I am thoroughly convinced that this is something that must be dealt with first by African-Americans. We have left the inner cities. Many of us have lost contact. Many of us should consider moving back. This is not a blanket command; this is a heartfelt questioning. There are many issues to consider: Our cities are not safe. The schools are not good. The housing stock is dilapidated. Unless people, black and white, are willing to sacrifice themselves for their fellow man, how will things change?

I do not know anyone who has been born and raised in America who does not now have racism on his or her heart. It is so effusive in our culture. I do not know anybody, black or white, without some vestiges of racism. The person I am most skeptical of is the one who says, "Kay, I do not understand all of this stuff about racism. I've never been a racist. And I have never had any racist feelings." I back away away from people like that. I do not accept that. I find it difficult to believe. If those people watched TV, read books, read newspapers, listened to music, they absorbed the undercurrents of racism in America. The first step toward reconciliation is the acknowledgment of where we are. The reality is: If you are not willing to admit that and start with that premise, then there is little that you can do to change.

It is amazing to me how dishonest some people are willing to be with themselves. Our challenge is to be real and honest. People try to change behaviors first. If you have a core, certain behaviors come out of that core. To try to attack each manifestation, each behavior, is akin to playing the game "Wacky Gator." In that game, you have a padded mallet and are confronted with four alligators that come out of their caves to attack you. You can get them first by pounding on their heads with the mallet, but the reality is that no matter how fast you are, more gators get you than are gotten by you. If only we could change our cores, change the *hearts* of the gators, then we would not have to beat them upside the head!

Some people in America are more racist than others, but we *all* have *some* racial propensity. Once that propensity is acknowledged, there can be reconciliation, forgiveness, and *healing*. As an individual, once I have recognized what lives inside me, I can start to get it out. I can pray about it, turn it over to God, and revel in His healing ways. I can try to deal with it in personal relationships. In work, church, and community relationships, I can try to acknowledge the reality of my racial bias. And I *can* get over it.

That does not mean that the first thing I should do is get overly aware of race. It would not be helpful to anyone if I decided that what I need to do right now is to take a Native American to lunch. It is amazing how the everyday decisions that we make provide us with the opportunities to step outside our racial comfort zone. When you make decisions about where you live, ask yourself: Is racial diversity significant enough to me to pick a community where African-Americans or other ethnic minorities are welcome because I want that richness in my experience? Would you pick a school for your children at which they have the opportunity to build and establish relationships with children of differing racial heritages? When you move to a locality, do you consciously choose a church with a diverse racial makeup because you want the opportunity to worship with *all* of God's people? There are choices you make every day of your life that give you opportunities to break down the barriers of race.

Crossover Ministries is a group of Christian doctors who have gotten together in inner-city Richmond to care for those in need. In a definite move against the greedy self-interest that has come to define many professions today, they joined together in a concern for the urban poor. Today, they dedicate a portion of their time to care for that population. They started a clinic to provide free medical services. On any given day if you walked into their waiting room, you would see an overwhelming number of black patients waiting to see predominantly white doctors. Their commitment is doing so much to heal the wounds of race, but they have had to build that trust. At first, the community did not believe them. The community did not even *want* them. Celebrating their tenth anniversary this year, this ministry is *just beginning* to become an accepted and appreciated fixture of the Richmond community.

Their big breakthrough was when they reached out and touched the life of a dying AIDS patient named Jerome. A former drug addict, who was wracked with opportunistic infections ravaging his body, Jerome spread the word that "these people are real." These doctors are making an impact on their culture in an upbeat way. It can be done on a one-at-a-time basis with individuals, families, churches, and doctors.

If overcoming racism is important to you, I hope I have made it clear to you what *you* can do.

Chapter Twelve

Poverty

> *The King will reply, "I tell you the truth, whatever you did for one of the least of these brothers of mine, you did for me."*
>
> —JESUS CHRIST

"Go to sleep!"

"I can't, Mama—the bugs are gonna get me."

"Go to sleep!!"

"I'm scared, Mama! Why can't we go home?!"

"We are home, child, we are home."

She was so scared of the bugs. Their old home did not have any of those roaches, but in this housing project there were hundreds. She had brushed her teeth, gotten down on her knees and said her prayers, then engaged in the last part of her nightly ritual. She pulled back the sheets, shook them out one by one, placing the "safe" sheets around her neck. Once they were placed safely back on the bed, she pulled the pillow from its case, shook out the pillow, and turned the case inside out. Inevitably in this process, she would find a wayward roach, or more likely, the wayward roaches.

This night, she simply could not take it anymore. She feared that if she closed her eyes and fell asleep, one of the slimy brown creepers would fall from the ceiling and crawl around her face, hoping to find a place to nest. She did not like this new home.

Mama had finally taken the kids away—away from a drunken dad and away from an old home. The new family home was a five-room townhouse apartment defined by rough gray cinder-block walls met with an equally dreary concrete floor. It was damp in the winter, stifling in the summer. But they would make do.

There are many people who believe that poverty is not a problem in America. Or that if there are poor people, they are only poor because they have not "picked themselves" up by their bootstraps and gotten a job—gotten enough money to live. There is also a pernicious stereotype that paints America's poor as cunning and mischievous, master manipulators of "the system," making money but not declaring it, living on welfare, and driving a Cadillac. While there is certainly some truth in all of these statements, it would be disingenuous to say that there are not people in America today who go to bed hungry, go out in the winter without adequate clothing, do not get sufficient medical care—people who are quite simply "poor."

By "poor," I am not talking about any kind of poor other than economic and material poverty. Entire books have, could have been, and should have been written about the richness in spirit of many of the most materially poor. But what we confront together here is the poverty of many Americans amidst the plenty of the world's greatest economic superpower.

The statistics verify this:

In 1965, when President Johnson launched the "war on poverty," there were approximately 14.7 million children in poverty, constituting about one of every five children in America. Five trillion dollars and twenty-nine years later, there are

14.6 million children in poverty who constitute a little more than one in every five American children. *Of all age groups, children are the most likely to be poor.*

In 1991, a study of the poverty rates in eight industrialized nations revealed that American children were almost three times as likely to be poor as children from the other nations studied. Who are these poor? Well, more than half of them are white. About half live in rural or suburban areas. About one in three lives with two parents, and about one in five lives in a family with an adult who works full-time. It is also important to remember that while there are more white children than black children who are poor, the percentage of poor black children is significantly higher than the percentage of poor white children. Specifically, black children are almost three times as likely to be poor than white children. Of all black children, almost forty-five percent live in poverty, compared with about thirty-eight percent of Hispanic children and slightly more than eleven percent of white children.

I know of what I speak. On many different levels. When Charles and I were first married, we quickly had a family of five, massive doctor bills, and limited resources. We had gone from two incomes to one, from double income and no kids to one income and more kids than we could possibly handle. It was not that we were irresponsible—we were disciplined in our use of contraceptives. It was just that our plans did not happen to coincide with God's plans. My house was a wreck. I was exhausted all the time. We did not have any money. I was wearing all of Charles's clothes because I had not lost my pregnancy weight and we could not afford to buy new ones. Once again, I found myself on the receiving end of charity. This time, though, it was especially hard. While so many good and kind people gave us money, clothes, tips on child-rearing and marriage saving, I felt guilty. I felt that we were poor, therefore we should be eating franks and beans. But at the same time, I knew how important proper nutrition is for the kids' health, and I wanted to give them fruits and vegetables, poultry and meat, whole grains and pasta. I wanted them to be healthy. And, believe it or not, healthy foods cost more.

Someone could have easily looked in on our life and said, "They're not poor, they're irresponsible. They aren't saving their money, she isn't working, they're spending it on lavish meals." They may have been right. But the point is, different people make different choices about what they do with their time, or their money. Those choices do not make them any more rich— they are merely the choices of people.

We have come, finally, to the persistent and painful problem of poverty amidst prosperity. We have created in this country material wealth that is unparalleled in human history. We are the greatest economic power ever to inhabit this earth. Some even contend that our poor live better than does the middle class in Europe. That is, however, small consolation to those people trapped in poverty amidst decadent wealth. Our Lord reminded us that the poor have always been and will always be among us. A quick perusal of the Scriptures will also reveal that Christ spoke more about the need to care for the poor among us than about any other topic.

It is fitting, then, that we close with the subject of poverty, for it is in fashioning a way to deal with poverty that we will be forced to confront *every single aspect of our lives*. With abortion, homosexuality, and racism, some parts of the village had a greater role than others. In each there is the need for some real navel gazing. To work toward cultural change in those issues, we are first required to look at our own souls, our own hearts, before we can look outward. There were certain things that families and communities could do in each of those areas to affect change, but it is, finally, in the area of poverty that every single resource we have—every ounce of energy and determination we possess—will be summoned, because to look at poverty in America today is to realize that to end it, we must reinvent the village that deals with it.

The first step, however, is not a step to policy. It is a step toward looking at ourselves. As we have done throughout this book, we must move to individual responsibility first. *Our* individual, *our* responsibility. We need to ask ourselves how we feel about poor people. As the richest nation on earth, we are able to live our lives without ever looking poverty in the face—without ever having to confront a poor person.

I remember listening one time at a tenant-association meeting in public housing at which they were talking to and chastising the politicians who were there. They said, "There is only one paycheck's difference between you and me." For the most part, they were right. If you go without a paycheck for a month, think about the bills that will pile up. Think about the collection agencies that will be on your behind. The mortgage company is very nice to you when you buy the house and are paying the bills on the first of the month, but it is amazing how downright unfriendly they can be if a month or two of payments are missing. In fact, they have even been known to kick people out of their homes. There is often a thin line between middle class and poor.

Face it: We do not like poor people. We do not like to look at them. We do not like to sit next to them. We do not like to smell them. They have a strange way of making us feel uncomfortable, of making us feel guilty. It is very easy not to have to deal with conditions of poverty.

The challenge of Scripture lays out a different plan,

however. As Ron Sider sets forth in his book, *Rich Christians in an Age of Hunger,* the Bible discusses many different categories of "the poor." Some of the Hebrew words refer to those begging for charity. Others refer to those who are thin, weakly people; still other words refer to those who are poor in spirit. The Scriptures also make it clear that some people are poor because they are lazy, and others because they have chosen to be poor for their own spiritual lives. But the most common reference in Scripture is of those "poor" who are economically impoverished because of circumstance.

The Old and the New Testaments actually talk more about the poor and the obligation of those with means to care for them than about any other single topic. God in the Old Testament is the liberator of the poor and the oppressed. The Exodus was not only the fulfillment of the covenant that God made with Abraham, Isaac, and Jacob—it was also the freeing of oppressed slaves. Recall that in Exodus 3:7–8, God said to Moses,

> I have indeed seen the misery of my people in Egypt. I have heard them crying out because of their slave drivers, and I am concerned about their suffering. So I have come down to rescue them from the hand of the Egyptians and to bring them up out of that land into a good and spacious land . . .

God cares deeply for the poor and about those who oppress them. Nowhere is it more clear than in the Incarnation of Jesus Christ. Christ's birthplace was not in an ornate palace that would certainly have befitted the first home of the King of Kings. His birth was not to a queen of this world but to an unwed girl. His ministry was not among the elites and the intellectuals; it was, first and foremost, to those who were *without*— without physical wealth, without spiritual wealth. His first visitors were not kings but shepherds. The first eyes to gaze upon

Him were not the mighty but the meek. His first caretakers were the animals of the stable. Our Lord's life, I suspect, is either one that makes us uncomfortable, or one that we tend to want to ignore, for fear that it will make us uncomfortable. Our Lord's earthly life is, I suspect, a difficult thing to reconcile for the purveyors of the "health and wealth" gospel of today. Clearly, Christ was not saying that all rich are damned, but just as clearly, I think, Christ was laying out the markers for our Christian life. These markers are, I am convinced, in different places than we have grown to believe they are.

The mighty men and women of Scripture were not typically the sons and daughters of earthly wealth, but when they were, like Moses, they had often experienced the tempering of God. Consider what Paul wrote to the Corinthians (1 Cor. 1:26–29):

> Not many of you were wise by human standards; not many were influential; not many were of noble birth. But God chose the foolish things of the world to shame the wise; God chose the weak things of the world to shame the strong. He chose the lowly things of this world and the despised things—and the things that are not—to nullify the things that are, so that no one may boast before him.

Of all the issues that we like to proclaim as near and dear to God's heart, whether it be abortion, homosexuality, or racism, God's Word makes it clear that issues of poverty are high on the list. If it is important to God, it should be of utmost importance to the rest of us.

But let us take a quick look at ourselves. How many of the checks in our checkbooks are devoted to helping the poor? If we believe that this is important, how much of our time and how much of our money is spent on aiding the poor? Let us look at our calendar and our checkbook, and we will get an accurate picture of how important poverty is to us. What percentage of the church budget feeds the hungry, clothes the naked, and provides for the needy?

Much work has been done by individuals and organizations to try to alleviate hunger and hopelessness of the poor around the world and in America. Groups like Compassion International and World Vision, and people like Congressman Tony Hall from Ohio, Ron Sider, and Tony Campolo, have done much but are generally defined as the "Evangelical left." They are differentiated from the "Evangelical right" that cares about abortion and homosexuality. Why? Why are the evangelical-right groups not concerned about poverty? Why are the evangelical-left groups not concerned about abortion or homosexuality? We talked earlier about how these issues divide the black and the white church. They also divide the political and religious left and right. For this there is no reason.

We need to present a united front, because what we confront, I believe, is an impending clash between rich and poor. History teaches us the lesson that as the poor get poorer, they get more desperate and more volatile. As Bill Pannell warned in *The Coming Race Wars*, we might find ourselves in a situation where the riots in Los Angeles are mild compared to the violence of a race or an economic war. We have an obligation. We have a mandate. To confront this issue, in particular, is not optional. It is required.

We need to be careful about how we use our resources so that we have more to share with others. We need to learn what it means to sacrifice—not to the point where we are so weak we can't help others but to the point that we feel it. This may entail forgoing certain things. It may mean that this year's vacation is spent at the nearest lake or beach, and not at one in Florida,

California, or France. It may mean that the new car you "need" can be put off by fixing the old one. It may mean that that big house you "need" can actually wait. We need to ask ourselves why we "need" four televisions. We do not have to go out and take a poor person to lunch for "Take a Poor Person to Lunch Day." *We need to reorient our lives from consumption to compassion.*

I do not think there is anything wrong with being rich or having things, but there is something wrong when all of that money is consumed on pleasuring ourselves and not helping others. This is not a sermon—this is God's command.

I do not presume to know what God requires of each one of us. But I do know that we have to ask the question, "If I really did care for the poor would that mean that we would change our lifestyle?" Or the question, "What does it mean for God to bless us more, to give us more, so that we have more to give?"

This is not a plea for the redistribution of wealth but a plea to *ask questions* and *establish priorities.* It means that we need to train our kids to be concerned about waste. Train our kids to *give.* Train our kids to be frugal and thrifty, to help other people, to be charitable.

To those who are given much, much is expected. We must be open to what God may be saying to us about how He wants us to use our resources. There is no doubt in my mind that God uses people with money and houses and things. The only issue here is whether or not you are willing to ask the question and hear the answer.

I am making no presumption about what God would have you do with finances or money. I only want you to ask the question and be prepared to hear the answer. God may be calling to you to a minimalist lifestyle where you are making a whole lot of money, but He wants you to give ninety percent of it away.

And He could also be calling you to a suburban house that costs $300,000. I can see how and why He would in either case.

Not only did I start my life in public housing and spend some of my early years on welfare, but there are people in my family now who are living on welfare, there are friends of our family on welfare, and there are acquaintances on welfare—several of them. I have a twenty-four-year-old friend who works part-time at McDonald's. Not too long ago she had the audacity to come up to me and say, "I'm tired of working. I'm just going to go on welfare."

She cannot read. She cannot write. She is unable to draft a letter. She cannot speak well enough to be a receptionist in someone's office. The answer to her problem, however, does not lie in a job-training program. I do not care how good the program is, I do not care what buttons it tells her to push. This child needs basic skills. She graduated from high school even though she was unable to read, write, or think.

My friend does not have the internal fortitude to pick herself up, teach herself the things that she needs to know, and survive. We need to ensure that children like her have a place that teaches them the virtues of life. She may need to memorize the *Book of Virtues* by Bill Bennett.

We must end education as we know it before we can hope to address the crisis of poverty in our land. To end poverty, we must change churches as we know them. We must also end government as we know it. So many of our current government problems were created by people who believed that they were doing the right thing. They saw a need and moved in to fill that need. Unfortunately, they were motivated by a misguided sense of compassion.

We must end the community as we know it if we want to end poverty. Historically, most of the programs that the bureaucrats of the Great Society took over with the government were programs run by the community.

One day not too long ago, I heard a knock on my office door. I was late for a meeting of the Specialized Transportation Council of Virginia. Much to my surprise, I also learned that I was chairing the meeting. Even more to my surprise, I walked into the conference room only to be confronted by massive briefing books that explained that this council provides for the transportation needs of those who cannot use public transportation. It cares for the disabled, sick, and elderly to provide rides to the doctors' offices for such things as chemotherapy or dialysis, rides to the grocery store for food, or rides to the mall so that people can shop for clothes.

The members of this council spoke eloquently about the need that exists to take people to a doctor. They relayed in particular the story of an elderly woman living in a section of Richmond, who had no family, no one to care for her as she slowly died from cancer. This council did all that they could for her.

They also came requesting more money so that they could meet the needs. What could I do? Could I be so insensitive and uncaring that I would turn away dollars from this program? If we want to end the plight of the poor and sick, we must change the community as we know it. Government cannot do all that people want it to do. The pie simply cannot expand any more. Even if the government could do all we want it to, all we would end up with is a bidding war for limited dollars with one need competing against another. It is heart disease versus cancer. Or cancer versus AIDS. It is the elderly versus the children. It is the education establishment versus the welfare bureaucracy. The government not only has limited resources, it has limited power to effect change. The community, however, has an infinite ability to change.

Why is that woman in Richmond alone? Where are the neighbors? Where *are* her children? Where are the churches? Where are the civic organizations? Where are those institutions that have historically made America what she is? What does this say about the village? What does it say about America?

All of the government programs in the world, no matter what they cost, will not lift her out of poverty. There are certain kinds of people who get lifted out of poverty. I hope that my friend will be one of those people, but right now she is not. Right now she is in desperate need of training in the basic attributes for a healthy life. She can get these things, but she cannot get them from government.

The great tragedy is that there are millions of boys and girls like my friend living in America today. It is our duty, the duty of our village to care for them. What we want for them is not a job handed to them on a platter. What we want for them, what they want for themselves, is the self-esteem and sense of worth that comes with having the skills necessary to compete for a private-sector job and actually get it. What they want, or what they should want, is nothing less than that.

Well, that does not sound very compassionate. Well, that sure sounds paternalistic. Well, it might be.

Individual commitment. Family commitment. Community commitment. Educational commitment. Cultural change.

Chapter Thirteen

Time Is Not
a Measure of Success

It was late July, and he was growing weaker. Though not fully alert, he knew. Talk of the things of heaven steadily overtook the talk of the things of earth. Then the word came. Late on Friday, July 26, the Abolition of Slavery had passed its Third Reading in the House of Commons. That meant only one thing: Slavery, as a legal state in the empire of Britain, was dead. Passage in the House of Lords was assured. This time there would be no last-minute changes. Slavery was dead. So soon would he be.

"Thank God," he exclaimed, "that I have lived to witness a day in which England is willing to give twenty million sterling for the abolition of slavery."

His health appeared to be improving. His friends found him lively and cheerful. He had seen the completion of his life's work. He had seen the vision that God had given him so very long ago come to bear fruit.

It had begun with a bonfire in the middle of August, fifty-three years ago. An ox on a spit. Drinking, dancing, merriment. The ladies eyed the young man who would soon win the general election. He was brash, wealthy, the son of privilege, and a child of a world with nary a concern. No one could guess that this man would achieve his fame as a man of God, dedicated to wiping out what he, and few others, viewed as a horrid aberration of the dignity of God's created life. On that evening, he was the host begging for votes.

School had been tolerable, made easier though with his wit and his voice. Both served him well. It was the Prince of Wales who said that he would travel long and far just to hear the voice of the young man. Cambridge also provided an opportunity for him to meet another young man with political aspirations, one William Pitt, future prime minister.

Amidst the ease and leisure of a life of political ambition and social pleasure were the cogs of the great industrial machine. For this was not only the England of the very wealthy, this was the England of horrid child-labor. Of eighteen-hour days and nights in dark, squalid conditions. Of children being sold to the highest bidder. For these unfortunate masses, life was indeed, nasty, brutal, and short.

There were other cogs in the machine, though, and for them life was, if possible, even worse. One of these cogs came simply to be known as the "institution." It was comprised of "goods and chattels." They were the slaves. Forcibly removed from their homes continents away, they were neither loved nor loathed, except insofar as they brought wealth and gain to their owners and their new country. Their existence and their importation was one of the three vital legs of the Triangle Trade.

A trip to the continent following his election to represent York-shire, the largest and most influential constituency in the country, would change his life. There, through intellectual honesty and an open heart, the young man came face-to-face with the person of Jesus Christ.

Much to his surprise, it changed him unalterably. Letters to friends and family revealed a changed man. He awoke each morning to pray. Soon, "spiritual anguish" engulfed him. He thought of his friends—of how they might view him. He saw that he had been a moral man but shaped by the shapeless idleness of futility and selfishness. Plagued by the confrontation with the Cross, he weighed his resignation from politics.

At the urging of his good friend, now Prime Minister Pitt, he reconsidered. And he sought counsel from his boyhood hero, John Newton. The former slave trader, lyricist of the hymn "Amazing Grace," was now sixty years old and the Rector of St. Mary Woolnoth in the City. Newton had experienced the contempt of the fashionable world that looked at him and other evangelicals with contempt, suspicion, and fear. They were derisively called the "enthusiasts."

After walking around his house twice and pleading with Newton for secrecy, he found the advice he was looking for. "It is hoped," said Newton, "and believed that the Lord has raised you up for the good of His church and for the good of the nation."

William Wilberforce took the words to heart. He would write in one of his many notes to himself, "A man who acts from the principles I profess reflects that he is to give an account of his political conduct at the judgment seat of Christ." His uncertainty and doubt was tempered into a lifelong determination to fulfill what God had put before him. "Almighty God has set before me two great objectives. The abolition of the slave trade and the reformation of manners [morals]."

Allying friends and persuading foes, he began his drive in 1787. His friend the Prime Minister relied on his detailed work and facts to persuade the House to agree to discuss the abolition of the slave trade the next year.

From there the fight began. The stories about the inhumane conditions of the slave ships moved from a distant fiction to an unalterable reality. Equipped with maps and diagrams and facts, Wilberforce presented his case. Opposition was stiff. "Two-thirds of the commerce of this country depends on the slave trade," said one *lord. Angered by rhetoric of the opposition, the once-ambivalent prime minister pushed through small regulations. First, an experimental bill passed that regulated the number of slaves that could be transported on a ship. Then, the fight grew more heated.*

The frequently unstated hostility to the "enthusiasts" and their morality became a stated hostility to the "enthusiasts" and their morality. One earl said, "Humanity is a private feeling, not a public principle to act upon." Another lord angrily sniffed, "Things have come to a pretty pass when religion is allowed to invade public life."

Undaunted and even encouraged, Wilberforce and his band of men became known as "the men of Clapham," a community of believers and questioners. They gathered evidence and fought annually to win. Giving up hope for a quick legislative maneuver, they settled in for the long haul. To fundamentally change the culture, they fought to win the hearts and minds of their opponents. They also became a community dedicated to abolishing slavery and its trade.

The few men of Clapham soon became the village of Clapham. The home of Henry Thornton, Battersea Rise, was the center of the action. As more and more came to visit, live, and fight, Thornton added extra rooms, and extra wings to the house, which eventually reached a size of thirty-four bedrooms. This group soon came to be known as the Clapham Sect—though they advocated no particular theological teachings.

Year after year, the fight went on. Year after year, legislation was introduced into the House and subsequently defeated. Illness, injury, war, and even the opening night of a popular opera stood in the way of victory.

The battle was not for slavery only. It was also for the "reformation of manners." Through Wilberforce's friends at Clapham, the Society for the Education of Africans, the Society for the Bettering of the Condition of the Poor, and the Society for the Relief of Debtors, were all established. The latter obtained the release of fourteen thousand people from debtor's prisons.

Finally, after years of fighting and after mourning the loss of his friend, William Pitt, success was imminent: The bill to abolish the slave trade was introduced first into the House of Lords. A bitter and emotional fight followed, lasting a month, *before the bill was finally given the nod on the morning of February 4, 1807.*

On a snowy February 22, the slave trade waged its final battle. As the debate reached its climax, Sir Samuel Romilly stood and gave a passionate tribute to this no-longer-young man:

> *When he should retire into the bosom of his happy and delighted family, when he should lay himself down on his bed, reflecting on the innumerable voices that would be raised in every quarter of the world to bless him; how much more pure and perfect felicity must he enjoy in the consciousness of having preserved so many millions of his fellow-creatures.*

The entire House erupted in cheering and roaring. With tears streaming down his face, the man slumped in his chair, realizing that finally, God's vision and his commitment and the commitment of so many others, was to be realized. The motion carried—282–16.

It took another eighteen years for him to see slavery itself abolished.

Reflecting on his life and God in his life, he knew his time too was about to come to an end. Suddenly, his health took a turn for the worse. Friends again observed that through it all, he bore the mark of a man tranquil and contented. Late Sunday, he stirred. "I am in a very distressed state," he managed to say. "Yes," a dear friend said, "but you have your feet on the Rock." The old humility asserted itself one last time. "I do not venture to speak so positively. But I hope I have."

At 3:00 A.M., Monday, July 29, 1833, William Wilberforce knew, years after it had begun, his leg of the race was complete.

His legacy and his vision, however, are still alive. And live within us, they should. If his history and ours have taught us anything, it should be that *time is not a measure for success.*

Wilberforce is to me as he is to so many others—a hero. There is much to be learned from his character and his actions. I believe that his life and philosophy are worthy of a great deal more study and evaluation.

Wilberforce understood what too few of us understand today. To achieve his ultimate goal of abolishing slavery and "restoring manners" (morals), it was necessary to do two things. Before he could bring about political change, he had to first change the culture in England. He, in fact, changed the hearts and minds of the citizens while demonstrating in real and tangible ways his compassion and love. He became a credible voice in Parliament because of his credible actions in his home and community. He was able to eventually win the political battle because he and a few others in England worked tirelessly for many years to change the culture.

Why is this good news for us? Why should we be encouraged?

First because we have many examples throughout history of how a few individuals can prick the moral conscience of a nation and bring about dramatic cultural shifts. I believe that we have more than "just a few" such committed individuals in America today.

As an evangelical, pro-life conservative, I have often been accused of being out of touch. As a black, evangelical, pro-life, conservative, I have often been accused of forgetting my past. I have not. I have not forgotten the racial slurs, the spit in my face, or the pinpricks I endured when I was integrated into all-white schools. I have not forgotten being turned away from housing simply because of my blackness. And most certainly I have not forgotten my childhood and the pain of going to bed hungry and cold. But I have also certainly not forgotten the promise that is America. Neither should you.

Much of this book contains information that, to put it mildly, is sobering—but it is intended to be uplifting, not depressing. When Wilberforce was going through his conversion experience, it took him weeks and months to move from a position of abject humiliation to a position of extreme confidence in the person and the promises of God. So, too, we must make the move from our sobering assessment to our existing challenge.

That is not to say that we should not expect to win. As I watched the events at the schoolhouse door in Alabama the day that the first two black students walked in, and experienced the hate and the venom that existed, if someone had told me that just a few years later there would be a black mayor in Atlanta, Georgia, I would have uttered disbelief. So while it takes a long time, by the same token, it is amazing how quickly change can come about.

People were convinced that if we integrated the South, the country would fall apart. We tend to forget the depth of emotion that was felt. By no means is the civil-rights battle over, but think about the strides that we have made! Think about it— Douglas Wilder, a black lawyer, was elected governor of the Commonwealth of Virginia, and he lived in the governor's house in Richmond, the capital of the Confederacy.

Recently I was in Tennessee, visiting a good friend. He had

decided after years in the fray to get out of Washington, out of the rat race, so he picked up his family and moved. I was anxious to see him and his new home. As I turned off the main road and winded my way over small rises and around massive oak trees, his house appeared in front of me. It was a beautiful home. It was, quite seriously, the perfect house. It was home. A Victorian house with gazebos, a swing on the front porch, wicker furniture on the lawn, yellow with white trim, an oval door, hanging baskets, and a walkway to what looked like offices or a guest house (it turned out to be both).

He came bounding out the house with a hug and a smile. "Great to see you again, Kay! Welcome to Tennessee!" He showed me around, and as he did, he explained what his life is like now. Every morning he wakes up early, puts on a pot of coffee, gets the newspaper from the front yard, sits out on his back verandah, and watches the deer play. He reads his Bible, walks around the yard, showers, and walks to his office next to the house. He works all morning, walks back across the yard for lunch, and then back to the office. I was incredulous. "We are up there busting our butts, fourteen-hour days, and you sit down here and live like this?!"

"Kay," he said, "thanks."

He uses his house for hosting high school and college kids. He puts up unwed mothers. He and his wife have taken what money they have and started a small foundation that gives money to inner-city kids, and on and on.

Look at the flip side. The homosexual movement in America pales in comparison to the size of the conservative and Christian communities. They make up a tiny fraction of the population, yet look at their impact. Why? I assert it is because they have a common ideology and a common strategy. They are not frequently torn apart by internal dissension. They have committed themselves to a goal and will not waver from it.

Think about the pro-abortion community. In just thirty years they have managed to assuage the conscience of a nation. In 1963, Planned Parenthood wrote, "What is birth control? Is it abortion? Definitely not. An abortion kills the life of a baby after it has begun. Birth control merely postpones the beginning of life."[1] Today, after the deaths of about thirty million preborn children, some professed Catholics are actually offering liturgies to "help women in their time of decision" about whether or not to kill their children. Their success has been nothing short of astounding. Why? Unity and purpose.

Why is it that conservatives and Christians cannot be the same way? Why is it that we are divided over matters that are clearly significant to some people but prevent the pursuit of God's command? This is not silly; it is tragic. And the consequences are dire. We have a nation that is now on the verge of collapse. Our historical institutions are in a critical state. Still, we sit by and watch churches operate as independent bodies. We watch conservatives battle conservatives and Christians confronting Christians. This is simply wrong.

A frequent debate heard in the corridors of Washington is whether the government usurped church responsibilities or whether the church abdicated its responsibility and the government stepped in. The answer, I believe is the latter, not the former. The modern church has abdicated its responsibilities to care for the poor, the weak, the widows, and the orphans. As a result, the social reformers had to step in and meet a need.

If we want to reclaim the credibility we desire, if we want to make an impact on the culture in which we live—we must give until it hurts. There is, I believe, no other way.

I have a crystal-ball theory. In our lives we juggle many

balls. Some are rubber, others cement, and still others are crystal. When you drop a crystal ball, it breaks; when you drop a rubber ball, it bounces. One of the secrets of life is figuring out which of the balls are rubber and which are crystal. In my life the crystal balls are my husband, Charles—my kids, Chuck, Bizzie, and Robbie—and my dog, Woody. When we evaluate our time, we should look first to those things that no one else can do. If I left my job today, my boss would have someone else in my job tomorrow. But Charles does not have another wife. Robbie does not have another mother. I am *it*. Members of my family may not have anyone else to care for them. Members of my church may not have anyone else to care for them. Sometimes when I'm sitting in my office late at night, I have to remind myself of that.

Our call is a different call. A few days ago, as I talked with someone about the difficulty of writing a book like this, he told me not to worry. "Kay," he said, "it sounds like you are beginning to reach the point of Calvary." I did not confront him on his bad pun, but I did understand. At the point where you are standing on truth and principle, very often you are standing alone. Or at least you think you are. If you find yourself walked on by both sides, you probably are at the point of Calvary.

To me, this is the reason that, to the men and women of the Clapham sect, Calvary is the great equalizer. All who came there came for the same purpose. All who come there now come for the same purpose: To die to ourselves and our selfish interest. To realize that the death of our King on a cross and His resurrection is also the great equalizer. It was the embodiment of where we must *all* stand. More precisely, Calvary is where we all must kneel and prostrate ourselves before the King of Kings.

---

1. National Right to Life Committee, *Convention Handbook (1992)*, 75.

Epilogue

I started writing this book in the aftermath of the 1992 presidential elections. Bill Clinton had just swept into town with the promise of a "new mandate." The "old order" and all of its people had been tossed aside. I was tossed aside. Hopes among Democrats were high. We were, it seemed, merely an administration away—this administration away—from a restoration of America's spirit and pride.

President Clinton, on a cold January day two years ago, said that he had come to reconcile differences and bring change to a stagnant Washington. It is safe to say that he did not succeed. Indeed, after the elections of 1994, it is not a stretch to say that he and the Democratic party failed, and failed miserably.

It was a strange feeling for me to pick up day-old copies of the *Washington Post* and read "Style" section articles on now unemployed congressmen and their staffers. I could see it in their faces, and I could sense it in their quotes—they were dazed, and they were confused. They wondered where their next paycheck would come from. They wondered whether they had a home anymore. And others struggled to figure out to which "home" they belonged—the one that they had represented, or the one in which they had served. I know those feelings well!

Unfortunately for them, the worst is still to come. The worst will come when Speaker Newt Gingrich, House Majority Leader Dick Armey, Senate Majority Leader Bob Dole, and Senate Whip Trent Lott begin to dismantle all that they have "accomplished" in their years of legislating.

I am a bit ashamed to admit it, but on election night 1994 and the weeks immediately following, I had to bite my lip hard to contain my self-vindicating smile. Finally, I found myself saying, The American people have had enough. They have seen the results of thirty years of liberal experimentation—of thirty years of "just one more program," or "just a few more dollars." They have grown weary of empty promises and failed programs. What they now embrace instead is bold, new change.

With as much hope as I have for this new Congress and its new agenda, it does not change my conviction that no election, no new law, no new amendment, no political party can transform America.

Real change must still come from transformed hearts and souls. There is, I think, a great danger that you and I will once again get lulled into thinking that we have done our part by voting for the right people—a sense that we can now sit back and watch these people write new laws, correct faulty policies, and get our country back on track.

The reality is one hundred-eighty degrees in the other direction. If there is one thing that this election has made abundantly clear, it is that now is the time for people of character and faith to GET BUSY! For thirty years we have been told by government that we should just send them our money and get out of the way. Last fall, we said, "QUIT TAKING OUR MONEY,

AND QUIT TELLING US WHAT TO DO." We must follow through now.

John Kennedy's famous challenge: "Ask not what your country can do for you, but rather, what you can do for your country" should be the byline to the GOP's Contract with America. For, while the Contract does indeed tell us what the priorities will be for the new majority party in Congress, the real message of the 1994 elections is a recognition of the proper, and limited, role of government.

More than two hundred years ago, the Founding Fathers grappled with the idea of federalism as they began what we call today the American Experiment. While they recognized the necessity of local and even national government, they also desired to create in the New World a system of government that cherished the individual rights bestowed by our Creator and that ensured that government intrusion would be minimized.

In the thirty years since President Kennedy uttered his challenge, Americans have not had to consider what they could do for their country outside of national defense and taxes. Instead, the federal government has told us over and over again what it could do for us. When it told us that it could replace the obligation of families and communities to individuals in need, we accepted this thing called welfare. When government told us that education should be administered by the federal government and that schools, rather than parents, should teach sex education, we accepted that. We even accepted the government's telling us that unchecked spending was necessary and that increasing the government's share of every taxpayer's income was necessary.

Today we know the full cost of ceding our responsibilities to the federal government. Despite the best intentions of those who created these policies, the government cannot be our parents, cannot teach our children about responsibility and character, cannot regulate individual behavior, and cannot create entrepreneurial opportunities. Bill Bennett calls our system "the nanny state," but I think that "pappy state" would be more appropriate since the government today is raising millions of children at debilitating cost to both the recipients and taxpayers alike.

The cultural and political change discussed in this book and by our new congressional leaders requires two very different yet complementary strategies. While our political leaders in Washington grapple with the redefinition of the role of government, we must continue to be vigilant in our homes and communities. We must continue to support and work for candidates who share our priorities; we must voice our opinions on important issues; we must vote.

But, these are merely actions in the political realm. It is equally important that we develop and carry out a strategy for cultural change. Cultural change must be fought and won in our homes, in our schools, on Main Street, and even in our places of worship.

The challenge to us today is indeed to ask what we can do for our country, and for our communities and for our families. Instead of waiting for political change to occur in Washington and our state capitols, we must have a Personal Contract with America—one that renews the individual's obligations in a just society. For only by embracing our core beliefs and working for change in each of our lives can we truly see regeneration.

That means that we, not the government, must take care of our neighbors. When it comes to welfare, we are the ones who must give sacrificially of our time and money. Churches will be called upon to become even more relevant to the world in which they function. In this renewal of self-government, it will once again be the children of God who will be called upon to lead the way.

Our personal contract must begin with our relationship with God, continue in our families, and extend to the institutions and elements of our community. In each area, we must take full responsibility and not surrender to the weakness of assigning blame to others.

1. *Transforming our relationship with God:* To bring about change in a sick culture, we must be a strong and fortified people—a people who understand both who we are and whose we are. If we are anemic and weak, we will be ineffective; or worse yet, destroyed. We must commit to transforming our relationship with God through prayer, fasting, fellowship, study—so that we may be equipped to run the race set before us.

2. *Transforming our family:* We must all recognize that if we achieved our goal of restoring America and yet neglected our own families, we will have failed in our primary mission. God ordained families and made it abundantly clear through His Word the priority that He places on family structure and relationships. We must transform our own families and, by doing so, secure the foundation of this nation.

3. *Transforming our community:* It is awfully tempting to seek to save the world while our next-door neighbor is hurting, while homeless people live on our city streets, while a sick friend is struggling to live with AIDS, or while racist attitudes exist in our community. If we begin to transform our communities—house by house and street by street—our nation will eventually become the great nation we all desire it to be.

Someone once said, "A new science of politics is needed for a new world." Today, a new covenant is needed for a new world. In fulfilling such a covenant, we can bring about cultural change. But, make no mistake, just as Wilberforce and others like him experienced, cultural change is neither quickly nor easily achieved. In some cases, it can only be measured in generations. And, though the cost is high, the result will be the real transformation of America.